DIANA PATTON
with Amanda Filippelli

inspiration
in my shoes

Inspiration in My Shoes

Copyright © 2016 by Diana Patton

ISBN-10: 1-944134-03-4
ISBN-13: 978-1-944134-03-7

Printed in the United States of America

Jeff Whitlock, cover photo

Nathan Walke, logo

PNH Book Publishing Studio

contents

dedication

To the love of my life, my life-partner, David. You are a gift from God. Thank you for accepting and loving every part of me. Your unconditional love and commitment to our forever union sustains me. Thank you for encouraging me to write my life's story and for being patient with me to finish this book. I know it has not been easy. I love you so much—till death do us part!

To CJ, the most disciplined and committed person that I know. I can't wait to see how God uses you with your many gifts and talents. You amaze me. You are such a leader.

To CC, I've got a question for you: Why are you the most beautiful girl in the universe? I just sit and stare at you, in awe. I'm just blown away by your love. Your sweet spirit and love for humanity will soon *wow* the world.

Mom, I adore you. Thank you for being the inspiration in my shoes!

To my sisters, Andrea, Toni, Janelle, Lola and Cheryl: I love you all very much. We are all different and I have been deeply blessed in some way by each of our relationships. Toni, you knew what I needed, when I needed it. Thank you for always believing in me and making certain I opened my closed eyes to the love of my life. Janelle, I always watched you and wanted to be you in so many ways. Thank you for being a shining example of a daughter of Christ, learning and always relying upon His Word.

Lola, my very best friend and my tenacious Christ-centered life coach: You are always on my side, but you gently push me toward accountability and lead me to a sense of hope that can only be found in Him. I thank you for always listening, *always*!

Cheryl, we always had each other and I'm so glad that we always will. No matter what, we always have each other's back. No matter what.

To my sister-friend, Rhonda, for listening to me while I cried in your living room in 2007 when I thought to first write this book, and for encouraging me along the way. Thank you for being the real deal. You, along with my other sister-friends, Jyl, Deb, Tonya, my other conversation ladies and my Life-Group sharpen me toward pursuing my God-given purpose with life-giving laughter along the way.

Special thank you to my friends, Michael and Sena, who believe in my mission and cheer me along the way. Michael, thank you for believing in me—you are pretty amazing!

And to Amanda: God put us together, this I know for sure! I thank you for your editing and writing gifts. You are brilliant and patient. You have helped me through some very difficult days to bring this book to life. I am excited to continue to work with you. There is no way I could have finished my life's story without you!

To all of the many mentors and people who have believed in me throughout the years by giving me a ladder to climb up: individuals like Betsy Riccardi, Jill Lancaster, Jim Klein, Janis Foley, Steve Dane, Dave Stratso, Steve Krull, Ed Zak, Rob Salem, Bill Rudolph, and countless others. Thank you for believing in me and reaching down to give me a chance!

Even when I walk through
the darkest valley, I will not be
afraid, for you are close beside
me. Your rod and your staff
protect and comfort me.

Psalm 23:4

prologue

When I am running, I am free.

When I am running, I am alive.

As I pull in each breath, I connect with a deeper part of me. A part of me which is reserved for God. An existential space.

Running is beauty to me. A well of gratitude spills over inside of me when I am running for not everyone has the privilege to run freely, or at all. Running feeds my spirit and connects it to my mind and my body. When I am running, I am whole.

When I run, I take in life. I think clearer. Inspiration washes over me and the fruits of this spiritual feeding help me to work out the emotional kinks of life. It clears away the fog and I chase down the path which leads to the truest version of myself. When I am running, I am healing.

I am running before I'm running. While I tie my shoes, I'm already there. I am already concentrating on the things my brain will be working out that day. I don't stretch. I don't fuss with headphones or my smartphone. I don't distract myself. I just run, both with my body and my mind.

When I am running, I feel my heart beat. I love to feel it pumping, pushing me. As it works harder, I breathe deeper and spread out my steps like a sprinting fawn. My mind and body work in tandem and I feel *alive*. I feel connected to my purpose.

When I am running, I am speaking with God.

PART ONE

CHAPTER ONE

backseat dreams

I wasn't listening to anything while driving home. It was dark out and I was brooding about all the things I had to juggle—new clients at work, my kids' schedules, my husband, writing a new lecture. In a way, I was praying. I was praying for God to help me with the sorting of my load. As I drove down quiet streets, I organized priorities in my head. I thought about all of the different ways that I would tackle the challenges the coming week had in store for me. I took this time to center and balance, to soothe the anxiety of the hurricane in my head. I took time to be strategic. But I also took the time to be grateful.

A red light halted my thoughts. As I slowed, I pulled up next to a dated hatchback with a little girl in the backseat. The streetlight glowed against her skin, her eyes focused out the window and into the distance. Her hair was parted sweetly into pigtails which lay still at the sides of her head. There was a boy in the seat next to her, rummaging around and talking, and a woman, likely their mother, in the driver's seat with her head in one hand, the other on the wheel. The little girl stared, unmoved. She looked removed from everyone else in the car, her thoughts somewhere far away. I stared at her. I couldn't help myself. I looked into her face and wondered what she was thinking about. As I scanned around her gaze, looking for some indication, I wanted to ask her about everything. *Are you wondering about the world? Are you wondering if it's better or worse than what you know of it? Are you wondering if there is more out there? Who do you want to be? Do you have a lot of friends? Do you laugh a lot? Talk. Are your words filled with questions and curiosity? Or, do you mostly keep quiet? What do you dream about at night? Do your parents love each other? Does your daddy love you? Do you believe in God?*

This moment, that stretched out time in the way that pondering often does, was punctuated when she suddenly noticed me. The little girl looked at me like she could hear all of my questions and we locked eyes with what felt like an understanding. I felt like I knew her, like I could feel her heartbeat. I felt like I knew that her life was hard and her burden heavy. I worried about her. I knew that she didn't understand why things were hard and that the world felt complicated to her. I could see a mountain of pain welled behind her deep, brown eyes. I could see confusion crinkled in her forehead. I could feel her desperation emanating through the window. As we stared at each other, into one another's thoughts, I wanted to tell her that everything was going to be okay. To keep looking out. To keep wondering. To keep dreaming. To never stop searching for whatever it is that she wants. I wanted to tell her that I understand.

Before I could finish conveying to her how important it is that she just hold on, the little girl lifted her hand and waved goodbye, and the car she was in shot away. I was still looking out my window.

. . . .

Watching Fostoria pass by outside my window always made me wonder if there was more to the world than this. Our small town is made of sinking houses and ivy-locked buildings. Beneath all of the overgrowth and dingy paint though, Fostoria is remnant of a town which thrived a long time ago. At some point, Fostoria had been a new place. A place you weren't born into, but where you chose to live. A place where the sidewalks laid straight, the corner shops were full of people talking over the paper, and girls and boys played freely in the streets. But that time is far away now—certainly before my time and even before my mother's. Now, everything looks broken and dying. The corner shops have been boarded up for decades and replaced by a cheap liquor drive-thru. The sidewalks are all cracked and piecemealed. The diner is closed, dilapidated, and moved to Findlay. Fostoria has become diseased. An infection has spread through the streets, the walls, even the people.

Although desolate at best, driving through our town made me dream of bigger things, a more fantastical life. So whenever my mother said she had to run an errand or go to the grocery store, I'd rush to the car to reserve my seat. With six siblings, there wasn't room for all of us and everyone took advantage of any reason to get out of the house when they could. I always made it into the car first. Today, my brother, Damon, and sister, Cheryl, made it to the car too.

As we piled into the Travelall, Mom pushed the gospel cassette back into the tape deck and we were off. I watched out the window as trees whipped by, people walking on the sidewalk blurred, and everything in the world became streams of streaking color. When you're eight years old, you don't know what else is out there, and in 1976, unbeknownst to me, the world out there was just as confused as I was. As the civil rights movement fizzled into more of a reverberation of the sixties, most people had settled back into their old judgements by the time I was old enough to recognize racism. Richer, more industrialized parts of the country were headed into a new decade—one that would come to be canonized by technology and diversification. But in that transition, places like Fostoria were being left behind. While the world outside of us catapulted itself into a new era, more primitive towns like Fostoria were left with the pieces. Without any part in major industry, Fostorians grappled more deeply with leftover questions about race, gender, and social progress. The divide had not yet been reconciled, and as a biracial girl, my place in the world felt confusing, to say the least.

When you're eight years old, you don't understand what different realities might look like. The world is still a giant mystery, but I knew that, whatever they were, there were bigger, better things for me somewhere out there. I was always the curiously optimistic one. Smiling. Laughing. Always cracking jokes. Deep down inside, I knew there were better things. I could feel that. I could hear it through Mom's gospel tapes. When Tremaine Hawkins sang out about "goin' up yonder," I knew she was telling me about a better place out there that God would someday guide me toward. A real place. And when James Cleveland sang praises to God saying, "I don't believe he brought me this far," I dreamt of the day when I could say the same. Those songs were about making it. About finding a way to push forward, to persevere, to go higher and higher, to not give up. I realize now that those songs saved me. That while I was sitting there, daydreaming out the car window, that I was learning to not only dream, but to believe in those dreams—to hold on. To keep pushing forward.

We pulled into the grocery store with a thump from the engine as Mom crunched the gears into park. She turned the music up a little bit and looked back at Damon, Cheryl, and I sitting quietly, obediently staring back at her.

"Don't touch the stereo," she commanded, as she always did. "I'll be right back."

"Get out of my face. You're disgusting," he'd always end with. It was my cue to turn and leave the room as fast as I could. So I always wondered, still wonder, what my father and Damon talked about in the front room. I've always wondered what he said to my brother in there.

The heat of it all was thick. The convergence of smoke and the heat of dinner was overwhelming. My father clicking his cigarette lighter, my mother chirping orders, my sisters quietly bickering, and the set, empty table in front of me—it all seemed to spin sometimes.

When we all sat down at the dinner table, it looked like a dress rehearsal. All six of us wore matching dresses that my mother had sewn for us. To save money, she'd buy a bulk of fabric from which each of us would cut out the patterns for our dresses for her to sew together. Buying new clothes for seven children simply wasn't an option for my mother so, most of the time, we looked like a small cult of matching floral prints and frills. If you think that I irritated my mother by having to peel potatoes with my left hand, imagine her frustration when I had to cut the patterns for my dresses. Being the only left-handed person in my family, in a world which left-handed utensils had not yet been invented, my mom often questioned my intellect while she watched me, tongue hanging from the side of my mouth, cutting slowly and with as much difficulty as possible.

Dad didn't eat with us often. Usually, he'd eat in his room with a tray. My mother served him like a king though. While Dad ate steak, we ate liver. Mom would call it steak but she wasn't fooling us. Sometimes she'd try to camouflage it by chopping it up, pounding it down, deep frying it, and then smothering it with gravy, but it still tasted like liver. Chewy. Disgusting. Tonight we'd made chili too and while Mom was taking Dad his special platter, we were having fun at the table. We all laughed as Janelle crushed a huge stack of crackers on top of her chili, then had to work hard not to spill any of it when plunging her spoon into the bowl. We played with our food and made faces at each other. We talked so much that we talked over one another, we made up stories, and shared about things that happened in school that day. If one of us ran out of food, we'd beg the next girl for some of hers. "Food for the poor?" Toni would turn and present her plate to Lola. Lola would, of course, share as the rest of us snickered and then did the same. When we were alone, we laughed a lot.

The six of us were bonded by something altogether different than familial obligation. Each of my sisters had been through unspeakable things. Things that I didn't know about for a long time, and each sister was compelled to take care of the next somehow. The way we grew up, the parents that we were given, the circumstances we were born into brought us together in a unique way. But I was confused by it all as a little girl. Sure, Dad could be mean, but my older sisters were burdened by something so much deeper. They had had it worse. Andrea, Toni, Janelle, and Lola, especially, had lived through a long, dark storm. A storm that had destroyed everything and left only rubble in its wake. By the time I was born, all I could see was the damage. I was always looking around at our family and wondering, *Why is there so much damage? Where did all these piles of wreckage come from?* I was born on the repair while my sisters had been dragged through the eye of the storm. Dad was tired from it now, and he was sick from brewing such a deadly gale over years past. By the time I was born, he was weaker, a rainstorm, an aftershock.

Tonight, Dad decided to bring his plate into the dining room and sit with us. When we saw him come in, we quickly shut up and sat up. Dad sat Damon down next to him and then looked around the table at all of us. His eyes were glazed over and suspicious looking. He scanned each of us, our place settings, and our faces. We just stared at each other quietly and continued to eat. Time slowed down as awkward moments ticked by. The tension made my stomach turn and erased my appetite. I put my spoon down after having finished the chili but not having touched the liver.

"What is it, Diana?" Dad peered at me, a piece of steak dangling from his fork.

"I'm full, sir."

I should've kept eating and not drawn attention to myself. I could feel Dad's eyes squint and look at me more sharply. He scanned over to Cheryl.

"Sit with your back straight, Cheryl!"

"Yes, sir," was all I heard from around the table as Dad barked orders at each of us.

"Get your elbows off the table! Come on," or, "Is that how you use a fork? No. Now, do it right." Or, he'd yell at us for talking if anyone tried to ease the atmosphere with conversation. Mealtime quickly became boot camp when Dad sat down. The pressure to sit correctly, eat the proper way, and to do all of the right things made our stomachs sick. It made even good food taste disgusting. Dad picked on Andrea a lot. Whenever she talked, he would shoot her a piercing look and scold her in front of us.

"No," he'd stop her mid-sentence, "stop lying, Andrea." It didn't matter what she was saying.

Most of the time, my mother would just sit there, slowly chewing on her food, watching. Maybe she thought that Dad was doing something good for us, instilling proper manners in his daughters. But I knew she understood that he was doing something wrong because there were times when she stood up to him. She once whipped a skillet across the dining room table at my father, missing his head by a centimeter. She was sitting in her seat quietly, brewing, and the moment my father raised up to say something, Mom was out of her seat and pitching the hot skillet straight toward his head. We watched as it flew by in front of us, steaming. In these times, something bubbled over silently and before you knew it was coming, my mother burst with a force that usually quieted Dad. She had the power to shut him up like no one else could. While he ruled with fear and intimidation, my mother was unpredictable. And sometimes dangerous. But she didn't exercise her power enough or with seemingly any reason. My sisters recount that before I was born, Mom once shot at Dad in front of them. Brandished a gun and pulled the trigger. Left a clean bullet hole in the wall.

I admired my mom for standing up to Dad even if it meant days of punishment for us all. It showed me that he was conquerable and that she could, if she wanted to, protect us. But I was never sure if the titan in her rose out of protection of her children or from somewhere else. When my father joined the table specifically to instigate us, like he was doing tonight, my mother did nothing. She just watched. But in other times, when my dad hadn't been bothering us at all, Mom would explode at him with a rage that came from somewhere deep and troubled.

We all kept eating, picking little bits of liver from our plates and swallowing it down quickly. I held my breath as I swallowed and tried to block the feeling of food hitting my stomach. I tried to focus on calming the churning inside of me. We all did. When Dad finished his plate, he got up from the table with a sigh and walked back into the front room. He simply walked away like nothing had happened and returned to his cave. We all looked over to Damon who blankly looked back at us before following Dad. As soon as they were gone, we picked up our plates and rushed into the kitchen to clean

The smell of burnt hair and smoke hit me as soon as I opened the front door. My sisters were sitting in a line in the kitchen, waiting for Mom to hot press their hair. She had Lola in her grip now.

"Come on and sit down," Mom whistled at me and Cheryl.

Lola's face was scrunched together as Mom pulled hard on different sections of her hair. It was a grueling process. Mom would set up the iron on the stove eyelet. One by one, we'd sit in front of her and have our hair pressed and wrapped so that we'd be presentable for church in the morning. Lola's hair was the thickest and most difficult. It also gave off the most smoke as Mom singed through each tuft. Mom wasn't gentle either. She had five heads of hair to straighten and she expected each of us to sit well. The hot iron would crackle and steam louder the longer it stayed on. Unfortunately, Cheryl and I were now at the end of the line and I was scared that by the time it was my turn, my hair would be burnt off.

Andrea had straight hair. She would always tell us that if we simply brushed our hair every single day that we'd have straight hair like hers. That theory never proved itself true after all of my tireless brushing.

"Hey, Joni! Why don't you turn on the air when you're frying the kid's hair?" Dad screamed to Mom from the front room as he got up to get a fan to take out the smell. He never liked when we got our hair pressed. He didn't have any patience for the smell.

We all looked up and over at Mom. Her face had instantly darkened. Pressing our hair for church was very important to her. If there was one thing that Joni Jackson was intent on raising her children with, it was a strong faith. If all else failed and her children were stricken down by circumstance, illness, or despair, it was my mother's deepest concern that we all harbor a genuine love for God, no matter what. It was by this principle that Mom took such offense to my dad's comment. She would not allow him to diminish the importance of this ritual for us. She made sure to show us that being presentable for God was worth the smell and the pain.

"Why don't *you* go outside? Then we wouldn't have to smell your smoke!" Mom yelled back across the house. Vindication washed over her face and she settled back down behind Lola and continued.

I just put my head down and waited for the inevitable eruption.

"Well, there it goes," I whispered.

My father came raging into the kitchen and all of us crept as far back into our seats as we could. Sitting on the floor, Cheryl and I scooted between our sister's chairs. Unlike us, my mother wasn't threatened by my father and I never feared for her. Plus, she had a weapon in her hand. They spit insults and threats back and forth while Mom barked at Lola to sit up straight. Dad stormed back to the front room and thick smoke from the front of the house came to combat with the smoke from our hair. After some time, and obviously hard thought, Dad came rushing back into the kitchen to hurl accusations and insults at my mother. The less she engaged him, the angrier he became.

This violent back and forth went on all night until my mother was finished hot pressing and rolling our hair. To her, it was worth it. Sunday was an occasion, and it would be treated as such regardless of whether my dad liked it or not.

I went to bed with my head still warm and dreamt about Gladys' fresh baked cookies and bean soup.

We were always in church. In the summer, Mom sent us to church several days a week to keep us out of the house, and when she wasn't working, she was in church with us. Bethel Baptist Church was a small, simple building with red brick and *God the Father, God the Son, and God the Holy Ghost* written above the pulpit. I liked going there and I wanted to be like my mom. I wanted to have faith as strong as hers and I wanted to commune with God. I wanted Him to hear me. I knew that I could trust Him and that made everything feel a little easier. The burden isn't so heavy when you have someone to share it with.

Dad never went to church with us. This was the one place I wish he would have joined us though. I thought that if he could just hear the Word that maybe he, too, would feel relieved and that it'd help him to get better. I wanted to share my growing love for God and the church with him and to show Dad just how unbreakable that faith can be. No matter what I went home to, no matter the hurt I felt at the hands of my father, no matter the tumult that comprised my world, I never questioned God. I've always felt Him inside of me, beckoning me to hold on for better things, keeping me strong, and showing me the path to redemption. Nothing my father could do to me could shake that feeling. God was my path, my light, and I placed all of my hope in His plan. When life seemed too unfair, too painful, I sang out to Him. Whenever I felt broken and scared, I prayed for Him to send me his Spirit for courage. I just couldn't be without Him and I wanted my dad to feel the same thing that I felt. I wanted him to feel relief and hope and love.

This morning's sermon was about Peter, my favorite disciple. Peter is my favorite disciple because he was flawed. Though he was an apostle to Jesus, Peter's mind lived in the secular world. He was humble yet offensive. He was honest yet sinful. He spoke with abandon, was strong willed, impulsive, and partook in the things in life that made him feel good. But most of all, Peter was suspicious. He was suspicious of Jesus even though he loved Him. During His life, Jesus relied on Peter to organize the other disciples, to reassure them in their faith. He was one of Jesus' most devout followers yet, when it mattered, Peter denied ever even knowing Him. From this, Peter's guilt bore some of the most beautiful epistles of the Bible.

Peter was a regular person with regular problems. He gave me hope for my dad. He made me realize that anything is possible and that love is unconditional. My dad might deny God, he might even deny me, but that doesn't mean that I should give up on him. God surely won't. While I couldn't rely on my father, I could rely on God. I love Peter because he was complicated. He wanted selfish things and he gave into his proclivities, but deep down, he knew that Jesus was God. The knowledge was still inside of him, just like I hoped it might still be inside of my dad.

In church, I was often silly and joking around with my cousin, Vicky, but other times, I sat like my mom. I mimicked her proper posture and her attention to the pastor. I wanted to absorb everything that she was absorbing. I felt a deeper connection with my mom when we were in church because she had taught me a spiritual love that I could hold on to. I was careful to flip through my Bible in the same precise yet gentle way that she did. I loved following along the passages with my fingers as the pastor orated them with such vigor and passion. We'd sing with our best voices and I felt free to express everything bottled inside of me. I could tell that for Mom, church was where you went to make sense of life. God was who brought meaning to things. For me though, I couldn't find that meaning. I couldn't yet understand why things were how they were. Nonetheless, church invigorated me and made me feel happy and warm and cared for. The Spirit was strong in church and I always left feeling refreshed and lighter than before. Sunday mornings helped make the rest of the week more bearable.

out of the hatch window to see where Mom was.

My heart had never beat faster. I was in complete disbelief that Mom jumped out of the car. I couldn't comprehend what happened and my entire body went stiff with shock. I couldn't be sure that she was alive. The car had been moving so fast.

I could see Mom behind us, lying in the ditch. I didn't breathe. I watched in awe as she stood up without a hitch, brushed off her skirt and blouse, and then moved over to the side of road and began walking. She had such intention in her eyes. I knew she hadn't yet given up the fight and if she was injured, she didn't show it. My mother is the bionic woman.

We were all terrified. But beyond terrified, we were hurt. *How could she do that? How could Mom just leave us? Doesn't she realize that she's leaving us alone with Dad? What if she'd died?* All of these questions started to rain down in my mind. I was confused by her behavior, by the brash and dangerous decision to jump out of the car, and I felt like she didn't care about us anymore. I could understand if she wanted to escape. We all wanted to escape. *Doesn't she see that?* We were all trapped. No one was free and no one was happy. So it wasn't fair for our mother, our leader, our strength, our heart, to just leave us so impulsively. It made me feel unsafe.

Dad backed up the car violently, screeching to a stop next to Mom. I was screaming on the inside.

"Get in the car, Joan," my dad called out to her through the passenger window.

Mom didn't say a word. She just kept walking.

"Joan! You're making a fool out of yourself. Get in the car!" Dad continued to yell to her, but she didn't even turn her head to look at us. It was like

Mom had gone so deep inside of herself that she'd imploded. She walked with such purpose, her brow furrowed with deep thought. It felt like slow motion watching her walk next to our car, all of us shaking with panic, my dad yelling at her to get in.

She continued to walk and I continued to cry. *Just get in the car!* I screamed to myself. I couldn't understand what she was doing. I was willing to accept a momentary break where she had to escape, just had to get out of the same space as my father, had to jump out of that car—I was willing to go that far. But now, she wouldn't get back in. She was abandoning us, leaving us to the wolf, and I couldn't take that.

I don't know if Mom felt my calls for her to come back or if she just got scared because we were so far from home, but eventually, she got back in the car. No one talked. Mom pushed the cassette back into the tape deck and simply stared out the window, away from all of us, the whole ride home. The Edwin Hawkins Singers just sang on, "Oh, Happy Day."

What was this side of my mother? Why was she like this sometimes? As strong as her faith was, as closely to Jesus as she tried to walk, there was always this sharp and dangerous side to Mom that was unpredictable. I knew she just wanted to break free. We all did, but I can imagine how her load was the heaviest. How many times had she contemplated just leaving us all? How many times had she started to run for the hills but turned back? And, looking back, she did run away a lot. She would leave Dad, always taking us with her, but something always pulled her back in. I'd wonder if she knew that I felt just as conflicted as her, but I never said anything.

CHAPTER THREE

part pinskey

In my dreams, I could fly. I'd start by floating around my room, close to the ceiling, looking down over everything. I'd glide down the steps and make my way into the den. Everything in my house looked so small beneath me. I was untouchable, up above it all. As I floated into the den, a black chest in the back of the room always caught my attention. It scared me every time. The chest had a presence that I could feel from the doorway and I knew there was something inside of it, waiting for me. The chest became my Pandora's box. Night after night, I'd fly through the same dream, always confronting the black chest in the den, but never opening it. I was strong enough to never open it. I'm not sure why I ever hovered into the den at all, but I did, every time, without fail. And every time, I'd leave quickly and turn back up the staircase, floating alongside the wall, leaving the chest closed.

There was an eeriness about my dream. A stark quiet that dimly hummed. Everything was a little blurred and captured in vignette. The colors were paler. The yellow carpet up the steps looked washed out and the white walls were tinged by fog. Back at the top, I'd look out the window. I could see the night sky and the stars shimmering above. As I reached for the stars, I glided through the window and into the chilly night air. I felt powerful when I was flying. I felt like I could go anywhere. I'd float over to the tree in our backyard and land in it. From there, I'd look over Gladys' house. I'd sit there and stare, contemplating nothing, clearing my mind. Everything felt soft and easy outside. Cloud fog silted around me. Moonlight danced over the neighborhood and I was the only one awake, the only eyes to look upon anything. I'd fly around the neighborhood like a superhero, looking down at the houses, making sure they were quiet and the children were asleep. The trees were always moving, swaying. I could feel the cool wind blowing against me as I soared through purple skies. Lastly, I'd head toward Field Elementary School down the block. I'd perch on the swing's top bar, leaving my legs to dangle, and look over the vacant playground. I sat there. The hall monitor of ghosts. Then I'd wake up.

I was always awake before my sisters. My eyes opened before the sun came up and I'd lay in my bed, staring for a few moments, feeling too heavy to get up. All of the weightlessness that I loved so much about my dreams dissipated and I was back in my room, staring at cracks in the ceiling.

The only other person awake in the house was Mom. There wasn't a day that she wasn't up by 5am and I'd gotten into the routine of secretly waking up with her. Although Mom had to work a lot of double shifts to support us and she had to be running on fumes, it didn't stop her from getting up before everyone else in the house to read her Bible. I understand it now. I understand that this was her time. Her time to be alone with God and to find the strength that she needed to make it through the day. She could've slept in but it wouldn't have done her any good. Being up in the early hours of the morning, at this unnatural time, was exactly what Mom needed to survive.

I crept quietly from my bed to the top of the stairs and slid down against the wall. I perched myself there, motionless, straining to listen to my mom downstairs in the den. I could hear the crinkle of onion paper as she turned the pages of her Bible. I loved that sound. So soft and soothing. I strained my ears to listen to her lightly reading scripture, and most of the time, I could hear her crying in between passages. She'd read and whisper and pray and cry. She was having a very soft conversation with God and that stirred a flurry of emotion inside of me. Mom had a relationship with God that I couldn't yet. I loved to listen to her morning ritual, loved to try and piece together an understanding of it. I felt the deepness of her sorrow and the expanse of her praise all at the same time. I felt the conflict that, every morning, she handed over to Him to help her carry. I carried that conflict in my heart too. In this dark house, at the top of these dingy steps, I felt lifted when I heard her pray. As much as it prepared her for the day, it inspired me. In a way, maybe I was intruding. She didn't know that I heard these secret moments every morning, but I think that I was supposed to hear them—that, in some way, I was a part of it and I was stronger because of it.

Mom worked overtime all week at the RCA plant so we didn't see much of her other than in the mornings. She'd come home while we were asleep and fit in just a few short hours of sleep before getting us up and ready for school. Mom rushed around while the six of us fought to use one small bathroom. Toni and Janelle took up the mirror while Lola brushed her teeth and Cheryl and I were still washing up in the tub. We were all rubbing against each other, rolling our eyes and snapping at one another in hushed tones. Andrea waited in the doorway for us to finish. Mom yelled for us from the kitchen to hurry as she was getting dinner together in the crockpot and putting her things together for work.

Dad wasn't awake yet and we crept down the stairs to make sure it stayed that way. The kitchen was still wafting with the smell of ground meat as Mom assembled the last pieces of her hamburger. She always ate a hamburger for breakfast. She stacked on all the trimmings and I salivated as I watched her bite into it. Mom set down her burger as we came in, washed it back with a Coke, and then put down bowls of mushy instant Malt-O-Meal made with powdered milk in front of each of us.

I just wanted a bite of that hamburger so bad.

The smell of the Malt-O-Meal was enough to make me gag. I pretended to eat it because I knew that Mom would be rushing out the door for work soon. As I brought the spoon to my mouth, I could still taste some Malt-O-Meal that touched my lips. Cardboard. Cheryl didn't have the same stale look on her face as I did. Weirdly, I think she liked it.

Mom lit a cigarette and took a swig of her Coke while watching us eat for a moment. She was so cool. She stood there, looking at us with a tilted posture, the elbow of the arm holding her cigarette rested upon her hip. The way she dragged on her smoke and then washed it back with her drink mesmerized me. She was such a mystery. I wondered what she was thinking about, what she thought about each of us. I could never read her expression. She was too complicated for me. I see now that she had been through it. That a lifetime of oppression in varying degrees kept her down but also made her tough. That her coolness was genuine because it had been earned. My mother was a statue, a monument to the hardest of women who had suffered through a couple of strange decades. While she ate her breakfast hamburger, she must've thought she was doing the right thing by making us eat this slop.

When her cigarette was out, Mom smashed it down in the ashtray, took the last gulp of her Coke, and headed out the door. We washed our bowls out in the sink.

I felt weary in school that day. It was the last period on Friday, and unlike the other kids, I didn't have much to look forward to on the weekends. Then again, I didn't look forward to school either. We were the only black kids in our school. St. Wendelin was a private Catholic school and we were there on a voucher. Though segregation ended, Fostoria was still trying to catch up. Our family was the first to be integrated into St. Wendelin, but we knew that had we not fit into a certain income bracket which allowed us a government voucher, St. Wendelin wouldn't have been so concerned with integration.

My seat in the classroom was in the back, nearest to the window. I sat on the periphery. As class droned on, I watched kids play on the concrete court outside. I could see Damon, a dark spot sticking out of the middle of the crowd. Damon was always heavy and quiet, making him an easy punching bag. His classmates were relentless. He was surrounded by the other boys, circling like sharks, poking and prodding at him as he spun around trying to catch them.

Damon was an easy target. It was more than just his skin color that made him different. He did everything slower than most people. He talked slowly, moved slowly, and understood things more slowly. Even at home, it seemed like Damon sat in the background. He was my father's child and I can only imagine how much that confused him. Damon had a quiet sensibility and an indifference that I don't think my parents ever took full notice of. I don't think they considered that perhaps Damon functioned differently than the rest of us. He seemed unaffected by most things until, like now, he was backed into a corner. But Dad coddled him so much that this was something he only experienced at school.

In a way, I didn't treat Damon much better than these kids. I mostly ignored him because, as a child, I felt like he displaced me by being born, by becoming the youngest. Plus, his relationship with Dad created a severe gender divide in our household. Us against them. So I don't remember a lot of Damon even being around because, to my own detriment, I blocked him out much in the way these kids blocked out his humanity. Realizing now how damaging it must have been for Damon to have shaped his understanding of the world around the things my father taught him in the front room, I wish I had treated him differently.

Damon was desperate. He knew he couldn't escape the boys teasing him. He never could. I watched this scene day-in and day-out knowing there was nothing I could do to help him. The teachers all looked away. I'd become numb to it in a way. I used to cry for him, but that helpless feeling became so overwhelming. Now, it had transformed into something else entirely. The shell of numbness molted, and on this day, watching these boys poke at Damon filled me with a certain fury. It became enough to make me stand up and do something for my brother. I kept watching, searing, as all of the white boys, mostly tall and lanky with crisp washed clothes draped on their pale skin, threw slurs and slaps at my round, brown brother. I could feel a tinge of pain with each jab they gave him. With an impulsive jolt of anger, I dashed out of the classroom, down the staircase, and out onto the court. I ran straight up to one of the boys, waving my small body around in front of him.

"Leave my brother alone!" I shouted at him.

They all stopped and stared at me with surprised, contemptuous faces. I'd interrupted them, loudly, and not knowing what else to do, they dispersed to other parts of the court. I felt good. I saved my brother. I finally did the right thing.

Damon looked at me with disgust. I was confused by it. I thought he'd be grateful that I finally intervened, that I stood up for him like I should. But

Damon just looked down and then walked away, disappointed. He wasn't happy with me. I chased after him.

"Why did you come out here?" Damon whipped around.

I was taken aback. "To help you," I looked at him, cautiously. I could see in his eyes that he was angry.

"I can fight my own battles, Diana," Damon turned away from me and this time, I let him walk away.

Defeated, I returned to class, confused. I felt such a mix of things. I thought that I did the right thing by standing up for Damon. I couldn't take watching him be bullied anymore and I wanted to help him, but Damon didn't want my help. He hadn't asked for it and I couldn't understand why he wouldn't want it. I stared at my teacher with a blank face as she questioned why I ran out of the room. I couldn't answer. I couldn't really hear what she was saying.

When the bell rang, I rushed to my locker, exchanged my things, and ran to the gym. I had joined the basketball team and Friday's practice was the best part of my week. While the other girls would meet up with their friends and crouch in the shade of alleyways, getting high or sneaking liquor, I'd wait for an hour in the gym for practice to start. I wasn't interested in making friends, and frankly, they were not interested in being friends with me. I kept a safe distance between myself and everyone else for fear that they'd want to come over to my house or they'd ask me to do something that I couldn't because Dad wouldn't let me. We all did. Everyone seemed so fake anyway. They seemed cruel and I just felt like they'd never understand anything about us. There were times I wanted friends, but I had my sisters. I already had some of the best friends I could ever ask for.

I loved to watch the janitor clean the gym floor while I waited. I'd watch him pace up and down, his shoes squeaking with each push of the mop. He was expressionless and he didn't acknowledge me. He just squeaked along at a steady pace until the entire floor shined. Once he was finished, all that was left was the humming of the lights. The reliable, constant, and dim hum of the giant fluorescent lights. With my eyes closed, I'd hum with them. The sound took me into myself and my whole body would fall into a relaxing slump. It was a meditation. It was the only time that my muscles went flaccid and my mind had the time to go blank.

A rush of squeaking shoes and echoing voices came bursting into the gym and practice started. Like Damon, I stuck out. I was a speck. But I didn't care. I wasn't focused on the other girls or their stares or their whispers. I was good at basketball. There wasn't time for the other girls to do much more than snicker snide comments to me or to throw an elbow jab out once in a while. At times, it was hard because they wouldn't pass me the ball or talk to me in the locker room, but I kept my mind focused on the game. Practice was rigorous and our game intense, probably more so because of the tension between them and me. That wasn't a bad thing here. I reveled in my work on the court. They couldn't best me so words were all they had. Their whole arsenal of insults and slurs would never be enough to take the ball away from me, outrun me, or outjump me. I was free then.

"What are you doing? You're always screwing things up," they'd hurl at me, even when I was doing everything right. And when they found that they couldn't insult my basketball skills, they'd move on to insulting my appearance.

"Why does your hair look like that? Why is it so greasy? That's gross. Don't get that on the basketball," they'd go on. Packing around me like wolves, snarling, and nitpicking at my differences.

"Do you tan or do you just stay the same color when you are in the sun?"

"What are you wearing anyway?"

When I didn't reply, the girls would whisper to each other just loud enough so that I could hear.

"I guess that's what people *like her* wear."

Questions like this were the norm for me in junior high. I heard it all when I was on the basketball court, especially at practice. These questions were insults masquerading as curiosity. They were mean and came with vicious intentions behind them—intentions that I could feel, that were stabbing. The other girls meant to mock me. They didn't care if I was an asset to the team. I was different than them and there was no getting past that.

I often wondered why the hispanic girl on our team who had tan skin and different hair didn't experience what I did. I guess she had a pass for some reason. But, I had to let it go. I had to keep going and keep moving on. I quickly learned how to ignore their put-downs, how to drown it all out. Soon, that became the norm for me too.

After practice, I stood outside alone, waiting for Mom to pick me up. I could hear the Travelall sputtering through the parking lot. I ran toward the car. I had to get in quickly while it was still sort of moving because if it stopped, it would stall. If the car stalled, my sister and I would have to lift the hood and crank the engine with a pair of pliers to get it started again, so I was always sure to carefully listen for the car. I knew Mom wasn't going to stop to wait.

All of my sisters and Damon were in the car so I knew that Mom was taking us somewhere. I fell into my seat and asked where we were going. Before Mom answered, I caught sight of a wrapped plate in the front seat and

I knew.

"To see Dad at work," she said.

I looked around at my sister's annoyed faces. This happened more often than it should have. My mother would pack us all up and drive out to the Union Carbide factory to take Dad his dinner. She'd even pack him napkins and a mint. *A mint.* Sometimes she'd make him a steak or something special from home, but today she'd bought him KFC and arranged it nicely on a plate for him. We could smell his special dinner the whole way out to the factory. I didn't understand why Mom did this. *Why does he deserve special platters?* I knew that we'd be eating some variety of troth-grade mush when we got home while Dad was licking the gravy from his fingers. It was so unfair.

I couldn't conceive of the things Mom did for Dad. I don't know if she did those things because she really loved him or if she felt obligated to, like they were her duties. Perhaps it was tradition, perhaps it kept things around the house calmer, but it was still wrong to us. Aside from the times she snapped, Mom was invariably loyal to Dad. When he got home from work, she'd make us be quiet so that he could relax. If we were too loud when he walked in the door, his rage would unleash because, now, he could complain about us *and* being tired from work.

"Buncha mulattos," he'd say, scanning us over while he put his things down.

"Listen," he'd lay into us, pointing, "when you all get older and can date, I don't want you bringing home anyone darker than the bottom of my shoe."

He was so easily frustrated by us and he'd point out that we were different than him, our own father. He pointed it out like we were less than him because half of us was tainted. We'd stand there at attention, quiet. We couldn't understand where the aggression came from or why he would say things like that. He made us. He loved the black woman who he made us with. But his comments made it seem as though he hated the woman he married. We were all so puzzled by that. It was like we were the results of some strange project gone wrong, the afterbirth of some sinful union. Even our father was ashamed of us—how could we not want to change ourselves? For my own sense of peace, I chalked his attitude up to deranged confusion.

Daintily, my mother would draw Dad a bath and fix him a coffee. She even dyed his hair. My mother did everything for the comfort of my dad. He got the best service money could buy and he didn't even have to pay for it. In fact, he didn't even have to earn it.

Once Dad was getting his bath, I asked Mom if I could run down to the Open Pantry and left, but I went to the train tracks instead. There were two rows of them that ran across Union Street. Built in the space between them sat a run-down convenience store owned by an old man who'd sit on the porch of the store, basking in the setting sun. I stopped behind the first set and looked across. The distance wasn't too far from one track to the next, maybe twenty yards. I started a timer in my head and sprinted forward as fast as I could toward the tracks. I lifted my legs and leapt across the first tracks widely, landed, and bounced back into a sprint before bounding over the second tracks, then back. Skidding my feet to a halt, *29 seconds.*

Again, *27 seconds.*

Again, *26, almost 25 seconds.*

I ran as hard as I could, and every time, I got a little bit faster. Sprinting back and forth with the wind smacking my face was liberating. Leaping over the great, brassy tracks, still steaming from the heat of the day, made me feel powerful. I used the tracks to train, to focus myself. I could run away in my mind while sprinting the tracks. I imagined myself sprinting past the finish line, a gold medal athlete. I learned to appreciate my body on those tracks and to want to make myself better. One day, everyone would want to look at me and want to watch me run faster than everyone else in the world. One day, people on other continents would see me run and win trophies and awards, and respect.

When that day comes, I thought, *I'll win as Diana Jackson.* I planned in my head to one day declare myself a full-blooded Jackson, to live black and to be proud. I didn't want to be part Pinskey. I was tired of people hearing my name and then looking at my skin and feeling visibly confused. Besides, most of the time, my father didn't seem to really want us just as much as we didn't want him.

I pushed harder and started to run more furiously. I had to get it out. Stomp it down.

The feelings I had about my dad as a girl were hard for me to decipher. There was something appealing about him to me, but then he'd be a monster. When I was younger, when we were all younger, my sisters and I were like little ducks with my dad. We were obedient and followed directly in his lead. There was a big part of him that tried to be normal for us. He'd always make sure we had a Christmas tree, and once in a while, he'd take us all to the drive-in, he'd put us in a private school, taught us good manners—he did the important things.

It was when I started to become a woman that everything changed. Eventually, I'd learn that's how it was for all of my sisters.

I was starting to realize it. There was a darker place that I felt my life steeply falling into lately.

Indigestion crept up and I stopped to catch my breath for a moment. I bent to my knees, panting.

A new dynamic had developed between me and Dad. One that was less balanced. He would treat us nicely sometimes and we'd feel like he loved us. For a moment, I'd feel safe, and in the next moment, he'd punch me. It was psychotic and there was nothing I could do but run it out. Run it out and envision myself, Diana Jackson, winning gold.

I am not white. I hate that half of me.

I took off on my fastest sprint yet. The sun was starting to settle behind the horizon and I knew this was my last chance to get the best time I could before heading back home. My legs were pushing forward with force that my feet turned into soft springs. As I cleared the first track, something caught my left eye. The old man was standing, waving his arms. I looked at him and I could see his mouth moving, but all I could hear was the wind rushing by me. He was yelling something. I cleared the second track and was smacked to the ground by a gust of air at my back. My knees stung as gravel lodged itself in the flesh. Loudly, a train sped by on the track behind me. The old man had been screaming for me to stop.

I scooted backward and gasped for air. Sitting there in shock, I watched the rest of the train steam by. The train had almost smashed into me, had almost ended me, all the parts of me, right there.

I took my shoes off on the porch and crept through the front door, quietly past the front room, and into the den. All of my sisters were there—Andrea was journaling by the window, Lola and Janelle exchanged gossiped beneath her, and Toni was flipping through a magazine while Cheryl looked on over her shoulder. I let out my breath and nestled in next to Cheryl. She coughed and cleared her throat as I crowded in on her.

Everything was calm and peaceful. We were all having a rare moment of relaxation together, decompressing and quietly connecting in our own ways. I felt secure having all of us in the den together. The air felt thick with sisterhood. I looked up to them all. Each of my sisters was like a beacon upon different shores, each one unique and enviable. I watched Andrea from across the den, journaling with her nose almost buried into the page. She was mysterious to me and that only drew me to her more. I wanted to know what she wrote about, what she thought about. I wanted to be statuesque like her. Lola, Janelle, and Toni glowed when they smiled, laughing. They blushed with girlish innocence, but they whispered secrets I wasn't allowed in on yet. They loved me. They hugged me and helped me when I needed it, but I wanted to be privileged with the older knowledge they had. I wanted to know everything they knew! And Cheryl. Cheryl was my rock. Though I pestered her too much, annoyed her more often than not, Cheryl and I had an understanding, a commonality.

In the midst of my thoughts, while I gloated over my sisters, the moment was shattered by the crashing of a lamp from the side table. It smashed to the ground with a reverberation that lifted me off of my seat. We all jumped. I'm not even sure how it fell, if anyone even bumped it, but the lamp fell sharply to the floor with a deafening sound. As it broke apart, the bulb made a popping noise before it went dark. We all stared, stunned.

I heard Dad's footsteps stomping toward the den before I saw him come into the room. He looked at the lamp and then around at all of us.

"Who did it?" he demanded. Dad kept a stone-like posture, his voice steady, his face unmoving but angered.

I looked away from him to the floor. No one said anything. I knew that none of us were sure what happened.

"Okay, fine. Everyone out," Dad motioned for us to leave the room. When none of us moved, confused, he gestured harder for us to go into the dining room. "Let's go! Now!"

All six of us jumped to our feet and scurried out of the den. I held on to Cheryl's shirt.

As we piled into the dining room, Dad paced across us, peering at each of us as he passed. I could see him brewing. The lamp had ignited something inside of him, had given him bait for punishment. It didn't matter how the lamp broke or who broke it. The thing was done, and Dad already decided that we'd been bad. He wasn't going to let us get away with something like that. This was an opportunity, in his mind, to teach us a lesson. To assert control. To punish.

"I'll ask you again," he started, calculated. "Who broke the lamp?" His words slithered out of his mouth, waiting to bite us.

None of us spoke. We all stared, silently. A sweat bead dribbled down my forehead.

"Kneel down!" Dad's anger boiled up and out now. I could feel the heat of his breath when he yelled, the anger steaming. I looked up at Cheryl, confused, worried. I could see puzzling looks come across all of my sister's faces. Only Andrea didn't look confused.

"Now! Get on your knees!" Dad screamed in all of our faces.

I watched Andrea slowly lower her body to the ground and get on all fours. She was trembling. We all followed suit.

Dad unbuckled his belt and pulled it out from his pant loops. It whipped as he drew it out. I knew now what was coming. Tears welled up in my eyes and I looked down to the floor, away from my sisters. I didn't want to know what they were feeling. The pit of my stomach hardened as I clenched my fists in anticipation. I tensed all of my muscles, waiting on my knees and elbows, like a dog.

"If no one wants to 'fess up, then I'll just whip all of ya!" Dad started and thrashed his belt across all of our backs and bottoms. Each snap of his belt stung my skin, singed it. Over and over again, he struck us. Over and over again, he whipped our skins. Over and over again, we screamed out in obedience, looking for it to stop. As he beat us, he humiliated us, loudly.

"Liars!" Dad screamed as he raised his hand against us.

"Yes, sir!" we all screamed and cried out.

"Good for nothing little bitches!"

His belt ripped my skin as it crashed against me.

"Yes, sir! Yes, sir!" we sobbed together.

"Which one of you lying bitches broke the lamp?!" Dad articulated each syllable to the beat of his whipping.

It seemed never ending, and I wasn't sure I'd make it through. Dad was relentless, ripping both our skins and our hearts to shreds.

"Lying little bitches! Who do you think you are?!" he'd shout and sneer as he reamed against us all with his thick leather belt.

"Yes, sir! Yes, sir!" I couldn't see anymore and my shirt and chest were wet from crying.

Then, suddenly, "I did it." I heard Lola's labored voice say between breaths, "I did it, sir."

Dad stopped.

"What was that?"

"I broke the lamp, sir," Lola was still crying. She hadn't broken the lamp, but it was in Lola's nature to protect us, to take on the blame, to end our suffering. I wiped my face and looked over at her, cautious not to bring attention to myself. She looked scared, her face still pointed to the ground. We were all panting.

"Everyone upstairs," Dad said. Sore and terrified, we all rose to our feet and hurried toward the steps. "Not you," Dad grabbed Lola. He was calm now. Eerily calm. I ran to my bed. ·

As I got older, I became even more obsessed with sports. By the time I was twelve, I knew that I wanted to be both an Olympic runner and a basketball star. My dreams were big. I couldn't sit still. My ambition scratched at me from the inside. I could hardly watch TV without palming a basketball or doing sit-ups. I was in constant preparation mode with a laser focus on being a huge star. I was always on. I was always thinking positive; that I could push past any obstacle and be much bigger than I ever imagined.

I knew I needed my parents' help. I needed them to recognize my dreams so that I could start pursuing them—maybe I could join the track team! I wanted to have something that everyone knew I was good at and athletics was my ticket. I just needed the opportunity to show it. With some hesitation, I started to bug my dad about it. I'd tell him how much I wanted to be an athlete, how much I loved to run, and I'd ask him to time me. He didn't pay much attention to it for a while until I think I eventually proved to him just how strongly I felt this conviction. He gave in. Sort of.

On Saturday morning, much to my surprise, Dad ordered me and all of my sisters into the Travelall and took us to Fostoria City Park reservoir. We rode quietly, my sisters were confused, but I was silently celebrating inside. I thought I knew what Dad had planned and if I was right, I would be so thankful.

We pulled up to the park and as we piled out of the truck, Dad announced, "Okay, everyone out. I want you to start running around the reservoir and don't stop until I tell you to."

My sisters all turned and glared at me. They hated me then. They always thought I was getting my way.

The rocks alongside the reservoir were treacherous. Each one was more jagged than the one before it and if your foot hit a rock the wrong way, you were in danger of them all sliding out from under you. Dad was yelling out to us to run faster and I could feel my sisters staring at me, plotting my death. But I didn't care. I couldn't have been happier. My dad was giving me the opportunity to show him and my sisters what I was capable of and I wasn't going to let him down. I ran with all of my strength. The rocks were stabbing through my cheap Kmart shoes and impaling the bottoms of my feet, but I didn't care. I kept running. I was the fastest of them all. I could feel it. I knew they didn't care, but I did. I cared a lot and I wanted my dad to care. I wanted to prove to him that I was good, that I was talented, that I was the fastest. I didn't know if I'd ever get the chance to prove this to him again.

When we finished, all of my sisters huffed their way back to the car while I strode behind them, looking down and away from them, but smiling. Dad didn't say anything about it to any of us. Even though he didn't compliment me, I knew he'd seen what I could do. He was there and that was enough for me.

Now I was hooked. I wanted Dad to help me all of the time. I wanted him to recognize my commitment and to see how fast I was. I hoped that maybe our run at the reservoir had peaked his interest in my talents so I'd ask him constantly to time me, even if I was just running from the kitchen to the front room and back. I wanted him to watch. Mostly, he ignored me, but I was persistent and I think he thought that to be both annoying and admirable.

As payment for my persistence, Dad started sending me out to run errands.

"Okay, Diana. You want me to time you? How about you go to the store and pick up my cigarettes and we'll see how fast you are."

While most kids get their one-on-one time with daddy playing tee ball or dress-up, I didn't know any different than this. I was desperate for my father to participate in this passion of mine and I was thrilled that he again chose to. I was so excited for the opportunity to impress him.

With a cigarette hanging out of his mouth, my dad handed me the money and said, "On your mark," and I got in stance. "Get set," my heart was beating so fast. "Go!" and I was off. I ran as fast as I could. I shot down our street, being careful to stay on the sidewalk so that my time was correctly measured. The trees bent over the sidewalk whistled for me as I sped by them and turned up the alley toward the drive-thru. If I cut across the road at such an angle, I could better my time by aligning myself with the entrance of the store.

In the beginning, there were lines that I had to contend with which really ruined my time. But after a while, the clerk knew what I was coming for and would have a pack of Camel's ready for me so that I could drop the money and pick up the pack without even stopping. I'd curve neatly right down the main street and hop back onto the crooked sidewalk that led to my house. That path became science to me.

"How'd I do?" I asked eagerly as soon as I hit the front door, panting, hands to my knees. My father would shout out some time and I'd think, *Shoot, too slow*. As desperate as I was to be better, I started to record my times. I was too naïve then to know that Dad had never been timing me.

Just as it had been with running at the reservoir, running to get my father cigarettes came to a less than satisfying conclusion. On the last day that I ran for cigarettes, I felt confident. Dad called me down from my room to go and instantly, I felt ready. I knew, for no reason at all, that today would be my fastest time ever. I could barely wait to get back and record it.

"Here you go," he handed me the money. "On your mark. Get set. GO."

I took off like a bullet, whipping my body off of the porch and onto the sidewalk, leaping over the faulty pavement and across the street. I dreamt that I was running in the Olympics. I was running for the gold. I envisioned cheering crowds standing in bleachers all around me. I was a track star and this was my victory race. The wind ripped through my hair and past my ears, my feet felt light, and my legs moved without thought. When I got to the drive-thru, there were no cars in line. I leapt through the store, swiping the cigarettes and leaving the money in one graceful, practiced motion. When I turned the corner down my street, I saw red tape ahead. I was going to burst through that tape, everyone was going to cheer and run onto the track as the judges called out my name in first place. I was so close. This was certainly the fastest I had ever run. The feeling was exhilarating.

I burst through the door with pride. "Time?" I panted.

My father walked toward me quietly and took the change, receipt, and cigarettes from my hand all while staring into my face. I tried to slow my breath, to stand at better attention because he was clearly upset about something. I couldn't. I had to take a couple more gasps of air. I was so eager to hear how fast I ran.

"Get out of my face," he hissed at me. I snapped up to look at him and caught my breath. I was confused.

"I said get out of my face. I don't want to see you right now," he spoke more slowly, with a cautionary emphasis that made me take a few steps backward.

Dismayed that I hadn't left the room, that I was still standing in front of him, dumbfounded and staring, he continued, "Get out of my sight! You disgust me!"

His screaming sent me running. My heart was throbbing in my chest but I didn't know if it was from running or from fear. Overwhelmed, my stomach tied itself in a sharp knot as I scurried into the den and away from my father. Cheryl was sitting in the middle of the room, thumbing through a book.

"What's wrong with Dad?" I asked her.

"Who knows," she said, not bothering to look up at me. I sat beside her and tried to start a conversation, tried to distract myself with her company, but she motioned for me to be quiet. I had interrupted her again. I watched her carefully. I was always trying to be close to her, to be paid attention to by her, and undoubtedly, annoying her in the process. I cracked a couple of corny jokes to get her attention. I made silly faces next to her while she was trying to read, but Cheryl just rolled her eyes. Being the youngest girl meant always searching for where I could fit in. Everyone always seemed to have so much more figured out than me.

In all the times that Dad disciplined me and my sisters together, or made us all work on something, all of my sisters seemed to better know how to survive it. I'd look to them for direction and try to copy what they did. Often, Dad would get upset with me and target me because I had so many questions. I was constantly pushing the issue and even when things got tense, I still wanted to be right or to have the last word. While I was scared a lot, I didn't harbor as much fear as my sisters, even though maybe I should have. My sisters had learned over time exactly how to do things, but I hadn't yet.

Dad took a strange and wavering degree of interest in his daughters. At times, I thought he genuinely wanted us to be successful, that he was striving to instill some set of skills and values in us. Other times, I was afraid to even be near him. The things that he chose to teach us, the lessons he deemed important, were strange and seemed so randomly selected. My father would become convinced that we were lacking in some way and hyper focus on that flaw. But he didn't follow through. He always tried to give us the tools but never the knowledge to use them.

It seemed almost compulsory for him. He wanted to kick start us down the right paths, but we didn't know where those paths led. "Sit up straight," he'd say, but then, in the next instant, push you to the ground. One time, he bought a speed reading machine which he made all of us sit around and take turns with. Every night, each of us would read aloud and be timed. It seemed so stupid at the time, but we had to do it and Dad would stand over us, smoking cigarettes and watching, one after the other. It didn't make us better readers, but we were too obedient to tell him that.

"Diana," I heard my father calling from the front room. The knot in my stomach cinched itself tighter. "Come in here," he instructed.

I looked at Cheryl before heading toward the front room. My heart sped back up and I struggled to walk straight. With every step, my stomach turned harder. I walked awkwardly, with a reticence, toward inevitable consequences.

As I walked toward the room, Dad was coming out of a closet at the end of the hall. This wasn't the first time I'd seen him huddled away in there and I knew to expect him to come out more deranged than usual. The closet was strictly off limits to all of us. Its slatted door was like the entrance to a mysterious portal. Dad kept things in there, secret things. Sometimes thin smoke would pour out through the slats, and other times I'd hear rattling and commotion as I passed by. I never questioned it much. Part of me probably knew that secret portal led to a Hell I wasn't interested in traveling to. But I was keenly aware of that closet's distinct ability to entice the monster out of my dad.

"Where'd you get the cocaine?" my father demanded, a rage boiling close to the surface.

Cocaine? I didn't even know what cocaine was. I wasn't sure what he was asking me at all and that had to have read on my face.

"Sir …?" I asked, reluctantly.

Dad's bloodshot eyes bulged a little farther, exaggerating his expression. His face reddened, "Don't get smart and twisted with me! The cocaine! Where did you get the cocaine?"

I began to plead because I didn't know what else to do. I begged him to understand that I had no idea what he was talking about. I could see my dad get angrier and angrier. I watched him tower with frustration as his body curled in, red and explosive. I swore up and down and on everything I knew that I didn't know anything about any cocaine. But it was no use. He came as close as he could and threw his finger in my face.

"Don't lie to me, Diana. I'm sick and tired of these lies and if I find out that you were hanging out with your cousin, Andy, I'll kick your ass from here to kingdom come."

"Yes, sir," I said. I knew to say that now. Just agree. Don't talk back.

"That's the last time you get to run to the store. You are a liar and you are a thief."

"Yes, sir."

That was the last time I went to the store for my father. From then on, he gave me nothing but suspicious stares. This one delusion of his catapulted our relationship into a netherworld of unpredictable, scary moments. The last time I ran to the store for my father changed everything between us. I knew something was wrong with my dad, and over the years, I learned how to better navigate these episodes.

This was the dynamic of being my father's child. Something inside of him wanted to be good for us and I always held out hope for him. But there was something that often took him over, his own Mr. Hyde would break free. Conversely, there were all of these moments where I felt so encouraged by him, like something had cracked open deep beneath the surface. But they were just that, moments. And my sisters had given up on those moments long before I had learned to. They were tired because, on the whole, my father was cruel and sick. No child should have to ponder their parents' commitment to them. No child should have to reach so deep, to fight so hard, for mere moments of what they guess might be true, nurturing love. His relationship with us was diseased, tormented, and sadly unreconciled, no matter how many moments he spent trying to actually do right by us.

CHAPTER FOUR

weeping willow tree of forgiveness

There is a day that will always exist in my memory. A moment in my life which both broke and built me. A day which I will never let define me, yet greatly shaped who I am. A moment both unforgivable, yet forgiven. The blackest of times conquered by a divine light.

As time went by and distance settled between me and my father, I was desperate to resolve what happened. I wanted to move past the awkwardness of his accusations and to get back to a better place where he'd at least pay me some good, positive attention once in a while. I missed him. As strange as that sounds, it felt normal. I was willing to accept that when he accused me of buying drugs that he was confused, and I was also willing to forgive it. I needed my father, so naturally, I sought him out.

Reconnecting with my dad wasn't at all easy. He had been spending more time alone than ever. He'd sit in the front room, smoking, playing music, alone with his thoughts. The voices of Marvin Gaye, Aretha, Otis Reading, and Diana Ross reverberated throughout the house. The walls knew every word of those songs. Some of them bellowed with sadness and bass that thumped along the floor, while others vibrated the walls with high pitches of excitement and hope. Being too young to understand most of the lyrics, I loved hearing him play "Me and Mrs. Jones." I felt like things were going to be okay when I heard that song. As I got older, as the nuances and context began to really make sense to me, I eventually found myself asking, *What's goin' on?*

When my dad wasn't alone, he was with his friends. There were men that would arrive late at night and my sisters and I would be ordered to stay in the den while they were over. We didn't dare peek out. The billow of smoke thickened and the smell of cigarettes turned into something fruitier. We could hear the music, the hum of conversation, and we could smell an array of things, but I didn't get it yet. I was the baby and full of naiveté.

I finally caught on when some kids on our school bus were getting high in the back seats. The wave of rancid smoke smacked me as I walked down the aisle.

"Whoa, that smells just like the front room!" I gasped.

"Duh, Diana," Cheryl snapped back, rolling her eyes. "That's because they're smoking marijuana back there. They're getting high."

Like a bag of rocks, it hit me then. *My dad does drugs.* As I took my seat, my mind raced back to all the nights that I would sway around in the den to Dad's music while my older sisters just sat around, annoyed and tired. I never got it. I always wondered what was wrong with them. *Why are they so miserable? Why are they always scolding me for being happy? Why doesn't anyone want to talk?* But now, now I got it. Nothing was wrong with them. Something was very wrong with our father and they knew it.

His brain was sick and he certainly self-medicated. Between drinking, drugs, and music, we could never be sure what state of mind my father had rolled into. As a child, I couldn't put a name to it. I couldn't chalk up my father's behavior to mental illness or diagnose him as an addict, but I knew there was a darkness about him that I suspected wasn't in every adult. I knew that, somehow, he was different, and that that difference was an ugly one.

The more I learned about Dad, the slimmer the chance to reconnect with him seemed. Findlay, Ohio was twenty-one miles from Fostoria and I started asking Dad to ride our bikes there together. I tried to entice him by saying that we could time ourselves and see how fast we could make the journey. I would bring it up any chance I got, but every time I asked, it seemed like he had forgotten that I'd ever mentioned it before. Sometimes he would ignore me altogether, like I hadn't said anything at all. The idea of riding our bikes together—racing down the street, the sun beating on our faces, my dad smiling over at me, the world blurred at our sides—was a beautiful one that I fantasized about for a long time. I craved the chance for connection, but over time, the idea of riding our bikes together started to become hazier and hazier as it seemingly slipped out of the realm of possibility.

I often spent Saturday morning hiding away in my closet, reading. Everyone was home and it was hard to find a private space. We weren't supposed to be up before a certain hour so I'd tip-toe out of my bed and over to the closet, shutting myself in until breakfast. The confinement of it felt safe. I didn't have to share it with anyone, and when I was in the closet, I could look through the darkness and see anything that I wanted to, real or imaginary. I could even envision riding bikes with Dad.

When we were called downstairs, my father was standing in the dining room, waiting. I was confused. Seeing him away from the front room was jarring so I stopped at the bottom of the steps and waited for him to say something.

"Let's go," he said, simply.

I blinked, "Go where?"

"Let's go for that bike ride."

I couldn't believe it. I didn't even move after he said it. I stood there, frozen with surprise. I had to take a moment to make sure that he said what I thought he said.

"Well, come on!" he thrust a hand in the air at me, and I turned to race back upstairs to change.

We didn't make any preparations. We didn't check the tires or oil the chains. We didn't grab helmets or knee pads. We didn't even take the time to eat before leaving. We just got on our bikes and took off exactly how I had imagined it.

The elation that came from looking over and seeing my dad pedaling beside me was overwhelming. We smiled at each other in the same way that I knew we would. I could feel the sun warming my skin and the wind brushing against me. I wanted to stay in that moment forever. I wanted to always be able to look next to me and see my dad, smiling at me, supporting me, enjoying my company. I wanted to hold on to the closeness that I felt on that bike ride forever.

I didn't worry about anything while we were riding to Findlay. I didn't think about the things that confused me, or the times we fought, or the fear that I usually had. I didn't think about any of that. We found common ground. We made a quiet agreement to be father and daughter, to cherish one another, to feel the sun beat on our faces, and to smile at each other. That's all I thought about.

As it is with happiness, the moment was fleeting and quickly morphed into another feeling that I was quite familiar with. Fear. After barely an hour into our trip, the clouds began to swirl above us and the sky was swallowed by an ominous shade of grey. The wind whipped at my cheeks and made it difficult to stay steady on my bike. Everything was mutating from sun-soaked cheer into menacing storm conditions.

I warily looked to my dad, "What do you think? Is it going to storm?"

"Not sure, but everything is okay," he assured me. He could see that I was nervous.

We continued on, but things only got worse. The wind began blowing stronger and stronger, pushing me off of my path. The sun had completely dissipated as black clouds rolled in and eclipsed all of the light and warmth. I tightened my grip around the handlebars as my heart started to beat faster.

"This doesn't look good," I yelled over to Dad.

He agreed and pointed to a large farmhouse up ahead, in the distance. To both sides of us were deep trenches dug alongside the road so we veered down and dropped our bikes. I immediately began to run as fast as I could toward the farmhouse. My legs were pushing as hard as they could as the sky began to thunder above me. The rumble of such a strong storm brewing took my breath away mid-sprint which is when I heard Dad yelling.

"Diana, no! Over here!"

I turned to see my dad, but he was so far behind me that his figure was faint in the distance. He had taken cover to the side of the trench, under a massive weeping willow tree. He was waving, yelling for me to run back toward him. If there was ever a time when I needed to run fast, it was now. The clouds began to swirl around and light up. A shiver came over me as the wind turned sharp and cold and I could see just how far apart my dad and I were. I had to make it to him.

I spun my body around and ran with even more speed than I knew I had. I pushed through the resistance of the wind and my fear.

"Diana, hurry!" Dad was yelling and motioning with his arms.

The wind howled all around me and I could feel the pressure of it up against my back, pushing me along. Even in a full-out sprint, I had to concentrate to keep my balance, to battle the force of nature against my small body. Everything grew darker.

Dad stretched his arms out for me and I fell into them without hesitation. He pulled me under the willow tree and tucked down over me, curling me up safely inside of his arms. The willow's branches lay drooping all around us, whipping in, out, and around with the wind. I lifted my head and looked up through the swaying branches. I could see the clouds were wafting and swelling more violently above us as raindrops leaked through the branches and splashed upon my face. I could feel my heart beating in my throat. The fear inside of me stretched into my legs and arms and stiffened them, bracing me. I was paralyzed for a couple of moments. With the rush of everything, how quickly our glorious bike ride had been destroyed by this storm, the ferocity of the storm itself, I hadn't taken even a moment to think about anything but fear.

Looking back down, I let rainwater drip off of my face and, as it did, it rolled onto my father's arms. It trickled down over his strong arms tied tightly around me, arms that I felt strangely unfamiliar with. My hands loosened from their fearful rigidity and I touched the rain dripping down these foreign arms around me. I explored them. My mind was pulled out of the storm as things seemed to get quiet around me, and then I felt it. Safety. I felt secure. I felt protected. I felt loved.

The rain started to thrash and the branches of the weeping willow began to violently thrash with it. I could feel the wind under my seat, trying to lift and pull us into the storm's grasp. I thought that the tree over us might even lift out of the ground, but through all of this, a calmness had suddenly washed over me. A serenity that I knew was impractical took me over as I realized that my father's arms were cradling me, protecting me. Although the world around us was rupturing and howling and flooding, I felt okay. None of it mattered to me because I had my father, my daddy, and he was there to hold me. Even if we were to die in that storm, I had a new sense of satisfaction. I had come to know what love and protection and safety really felt like. With the storm scourging and thundering around us, the love that I felt in my father's arms brought beauty to the darkness. I looked up through the branches again, but this time I smiled. When you've never felt the warmth of safety and sincere love, its first presence makes you feel invincible. I began to love that storm. I began to embrace the weather battering against our backs because it had brought my father's arms around me. In the depths of fear and danger came my first taste of worth and security.

When the skies cleared and the rain subsided, the sun came back out. Dad loosened his grip and examined me, making sure I was okay. We looked at each other for a moment. We were soaking.

"You okay?" he looked in my eyes.

I nodded, and we crawled out from under the willow tree.

Dad was quick to move on. We didn't talk about the storm, and he didn't look at me much again. He was candidly concerned with getting back home.

We decided to ride on to Findlay since it was closer now than Fostoria. The last couple of miles into town weren't the same as before the storm. We rode quietly, Dad a little farther ahead of me. The sun didn't feel as warm against my wet skin and there weren't any more smiles to be exchanged. Despite this, I was happy. I was content in the memory I made wrapped up safely in my father's arms under the willow tree. Nothing could take that moment away. It felt like no amount of disappointment could trump that warm feeling of security that I'd never forget. I have never looked at a willow tree the same.

When we rode into Findlay, we headed straight to Kmart. We bought some towels to dry off with and some chocolate to treat ourselves. Once we'd had a moment to pat dry and take a few breaths, Dad called Mom from a payphone on the corner to come pick us up.

I'd had just enough time to finish my chocolate before the Travelall pulled up carrying my mom and Janelle. It felt sad to see them pull in. I wanted to keep going, to ride all the way home with Dad. I wanted to extend this time together for as long as I could. I wished that he wanted that too. Looking over the hatchback, my dad said that we'd *have* to ride the bikes home. I could feel my face light up and I hopped back on my bike.

We rode all the way back to Fostoria, all twenty-one miles, together, and all the time, I reminisced about Dad holding me tight.

. . . .

In the same year that I learned about what love and safety feel like, I also learned about pain and the difficult act of forgiveness. I was never able to capture another happy moment with Dad after our bike ride. In fact, he seemed to slip downhill, spiraling dangerously and destructively. It was like I had gotten the last drop out of him that day; like I had used up all that was left and now Dad was just this unpredictable man, filled full of rage and suspicion. His mind had permanently wandered off and I felt no connection left with him; no way to bridge the gap that had been built.

My father had a heart condition and a substance abuse problem. Or, my father had a heart condition because he had a substance abuse problem. I'm not sure. But either way, one exacerbated the other and eventually, he could no longer work. His blood pressure would bottom out unexpectedly and he'd pass out for periods of time which made working impossible. However, being unemployed wasn't good for his health either. With the loss of his ability to work, very clearly came the loss of his hope. He became so wrapped up inside of his head that he stopped conversing with all of us. Days would go by when he didn't speak more than a simple "hello" or "goodnight" to me. After having come as close as I'd ever been to feeling the parental, loving side of my father, he quickly drifted as far away as he'd ever gone.

Dad began smoking relentlessly and not just in the evenings. He began taking more and more prescription drugs. His delusions grew worse as did his anger. Maybe because I was older now. Maybe because some of my sisters had moved out. For whatever reason, I became my father's target. He funneled his frustration into me. He took out whatever paranoid anguish he was harboring on me and opened my eyes to the reality of how sick he truly was. I couldn't deny it like I had for all of my life this far. Now, he was making it very clear to me.

On a quiet fall night, I woke up to my father yelling for me and my sister to come downstairs. I was confused at first, groggy from dreaming. I perked up for a moment and heard Dad yell for us again before I scrambled out of my bed and down the stairs. Mom was working a double shift and on days like these, if my father needed something, he demanded it from us. This time, he said that his medication was not working and that he needed help. When Cheryl and I peeked into our parents' room, we saw our father in bed, shaking. He said that he was cold and that we needed to help him get warm. His face was red and his expression strange. I didn't know what to make of it and instantly felt my stomach knot up with fear. I could see the same feelings wash over Cheryl's face. We'd never seen Dad like this and we were worried for him.

"Do you think we should call Mom?" Cheryl questioned.

"No," Dad was quick to yell from his bed.

"We should call 911," I suggested to Cheryl.

With that, my father screamed louder with anger, "No! C'mon over here and help me get warm. Cheryl," he instructed, "go to the kitchen and get me some water."

"Yes, sir," Cheryl replied meekly, and headed around the corner.

I stood in the doorway with trepidation. I wasn't sure what the right thing to do was or what was even wrong with Dad.

"Okay, Diana, I need you to come over here and rub my hands," he said, motioning for me to come forward.

Quickly, I rushed to my knees beside him and began briskly rubbing his hands. I wanted to do whatever I could to help him for I feared his heart giving out. He felt clammy to the touch, soaked with fever. He was sick and his body seemed to be freezing up. I tried to rub the circulation back into his hands. I looked up at him. His face was pale with cold sweat, his eyes dim.

Cheryl returned with the water and helped Dad to take his medication by putting the pill in his mouth, like he'd asked. I stopped rubbing his hands so that he could concentrate on swallowing, and Cheryl watched him closely as he took the pill down. Without thanking her, Dad sent Cheryl back upstairs.

"Go on," he instructed her, "I just need Diana to help me now."

With those words, I froze. A strange and overwhelming feeling rushed through my body, electrifying me with fear. I could feel something lingering in the atmosphere, something very wrong. My stomach knotted up, twisting into a tightknit ball that nearly doubled me over. I watched Cheryl start back up the stairs while memories of hushed conversations between my sisters started to invade my mind. I thought about Andrea.

"I don't know. I don't remember," I heard her say to Toni. "I just woke up and he was there."

I remember them consoling one another. I remember Lola whispering.

I hear Dad calling Andrea downstairs a lot too. Why does he always call for her?

Something wasn't right here. Something bigger than usual.

"Come sit here," Dad motioned for me to sit next to him on the bed. He pointed while I stared blankly. He pointed again with force and I sauntered over, shuffling with confusion.

Dad pulled himself up and kneeled beside me. He was shaking, his hands controlled by tremors. As he brought them closer to me, I felt terrified. Instinctively, I felt scared for my life. Something inside of me was yelling, telling me to run. I had no idea what was happening or what Dad was going to do, but the air in the room turned rotten and I started to pray.

"Okay, Diana," he spoke to me calmly and slowly, like I was a little child.

"I really need to get my hands warm and I need you to cooperate with me."

"Yes, sir."

"If I don't get my hands warm, who knows what will happen," he warned me. He looked down at me, shaking his head like what he was saying was indisputable.

Out of sheer desperation, I blurted, "But, don't you think we should call 911 if something bad might happen?" I was trying to save my life. I knew that then.

Dad's face twisted and he answered me with disgust, "Diana, I know what I am doing so I just need you to help me here, okay?" He was angry that I'd resisted. "Are you going to listen to me or just keep telling me what to do?

Huh?"

"Yes, sir," I put my head down.

I was trapped. I could feel myself start to suffocate as a darkness began to creep in; an evil that was sure to wipe away anything left that was good, now or to come. The way Dad was talking, the way he was instructing me was filled with sour intentions. He was corralling me, pushing me into an inescapable corner where my choices were submission or violence. In this moment, my world exploded into a million unmendable pieces. He was going to ruin me, like he had ruined my sisters.

Dad laid his head on my lap and put his hands on the outsides of my thighs, under my nightgown. The touch of his cold, disgusting fingers paralyzed me. His hands were doing something totally opposite than what they had done under the willow tree. He was no longer my protector. He had become my predator. Dad slowly inched his hands up and turned them down, in between my legs. He kept his hands there for some time. I sat there, shaking. More quickly, Dad moved his hands back to the outside of my thighs and grabbed at my underwear, pulling them down. I quivered in fear.

Dad looked up at me, his daughter, and asked me to lift up so that he could pull my underwear all the way off. I looked back at him, into my father's face, with a stinging hate that roared all the way through my body.

"No. STOP!" I screamed with all of the force I could as I shot away from him, pushing him away from me.

As my dad went back off balance, he stumbled, quickly got back up, and hurled himself forward, catching me, and pinning me to the ground. He put his hand tightly over my mouth, his whole face bulging and angry.

"Are you crazy? What are you thinking? Shut up," he hissed at me.

I was crying and I couldn't breathe under him. I looked up behind me and saw Cheryl standing in the doorway. She'd heard me scream and Dad was furious.

"What are you doing? Get upstairs!" Cheryl stuttered back and forth for a moment. She looked at my sobbing face and back toward Dad with fear. Dad let me up and backed away. I fled to Cheryl's side.

"The both of you, get upstairs! I don't want to see your faces. Hell, if I feel like I'm going to die, I'm certainly not gon' call on you two for help!" Dad threw his hands up and went back to bed, muttering about how terrible we were. He stared us down viciously, like we had tried to hurt him.

I ran upstairs and leapt into my bed. I pulled the covers up to my face and wrapped myself in them as tightly as I could. I cried into my pillow for so long I thought my face might prune. Dad had taken something from me that night, something that he could never make up for, never give back. I felt nauseous and dizzy. I felt like I was going to die, and deep down, I was hoping that I would. I wanted to fall asleep and never wake up the next morning. *How could I possibly face the world after this? How could I ever look at my dad? At Cheryl?* There would never be anything more deeply wounding, nothing more hurtful, and nothing sharper than the pain created in my soul when my dad used his hands against me. I knew that and I wanted to die.

I did everything I could the following evening to avoid my father. When he passed me at the table, I could feel him staring at me with a cross look, as if I had done something wrong. He called me into the front room with him, looking out into the hallway to make sure we were alone. I kept my head down, my eyes away. I wasn't able to look at him yet.

"Let me set the record straight here, Diana," he started in my face. "I don't know what you were thinking, but you could have killed me! Don't you know how sick I am?"

"Yes, sir."

I just wanted him to get away from me. I couldn't stand having him stand so closely to me. Nevermind what he was saying or how he tried to justify the gross thing he had done, I hated hearing his voice. I hated smelling him near me. I hated him. I hated myself.

Nothing would ever be the same again.

CHAPTER FIVE

inspiration in my shoes

In high school, track was the most important thing to me. I'd grown into my body and I was more agile than ever. I worked hard and never settled to be less than the best. My legs became trunks of muscle and my mind became a narrow tunnel, focused on running and leaving home soon. I was the fastest on the team and I knew that track would one day be my ticket out of Fostoria.

The more Dad tormented us, the harder I ran. Now, Cheryl, Damon, and I were the only ones left in the house. Andrea had run away from home. After a big fight with Dad, we never saw her again. He kept calling her a liar and wouldn't relent. I wasn't sure what for, but my parents never listened to Andrea like she needed them to, so she did what most girls would do at that age—feeling alone and abandoned, she ran away. She got out. I think Mom might've known where she was and just didn't make her come back because she never seemed as worried about it as she should've been. Once in a while, she'd get a letter from Andrea, and Cheryl and I would watch Mom cry while she read it. Toni made it big with Orther Foods and moved to Orlando to manage McDonalds stores. Janelle married an African-American man named Bruce and moved to Fort Wayne, Indiana. She'd gotten a job at Hudson's Department Store and was modeling on the side. Lola was the most recent to leave and she eventually wound up in Orlando with Toni. In their absence, all of my dad's rage became evenly divided between me and Cheryl. Even still, high school went by faster because of track. I was jealous of my sisters who were gone and I knew that next year, Cheryl would leave me too. Then I'd be all alone with Dad. The terror that thought brought kept me running. I ran straight towards scholarships knowing that college would be my only escape.

My classmates stopped teasing me as much in high school and I noticed them even less because of it. Strangely, they began to respect me more. They could see that their coups couldn't hurt me, that I didn't care about their cliques. I had been ignoring them for so long that they'd given up. Plus, everyone started to see that I was athletically talented and that earned me some esteem. I was a nice person who didn't retaliate against them for how they'd treated me in years past. Before I just didn't like them, now I just didn't care about them. I only cared about athletics and getting out of Fostoria. I tightly shut everything else out. When my peers voted me homecoming queen, I never thought for a second that it had anything to do with recognition, but everything to do with mocking me. I didn't take it seriously. While I should've been proud—*I was the first black homecoming queen*—I was convinced that everyone was just trying to embarrass me. I dismissed it as a fluke, and put my head back down to the grind, continuing to focus on my game plan.

Only running could set me free.

Mom started to take more notice of me in high school. She recognized my determination, saw that I had something special. Although she couldn't make it to my track meets, she wanted me to know that she was thinking about me. It was like clockwork. I'd tell Mom that I had a track meet coming up the next day and in the morning, I'd find a handwritten note in my shoe.

They shall run and not be weary and they shall walk and not faint.
Isaiah 40:31

Mom would leave me these notes so that I knew she cared. It was her way of encouraging me. She didn't have the time to go to the meets between double shifts so she used these notes, these pieces of inspiration, to connect with me in the important moments. She, too, knew that this would be my way out. She knew of my dreams to be a decorated athlete and probably imagined a life for me that had been impossible for her. Despite it all, I had a chance. Mom knew that.

Each note helped me get through the day. I left them in my shoes and walked with them. I let the scripture and her words of encouragement be what lifted my feet. During my meets, I'd run with a lightness knowing that my mother was supporting me. Even in the rain, I pushed harder when there was a note in my shoe. Every time I came down the steps and saw a scrap of paper sitting inside of my shoe, I felt empowered. They made me believe that I was going to be okay and the scripture reminded me that with Christ, by keeping a tight hold on Him, all things are possible. Even leaving Fostoria.

Let us run with endurance, the race that is set before us, looking to Jesus.
Hebrews 12:1-3

I was winning a lot of track meets and all of the coaches were sure that I'd go on to run in college. I didn't have a doubt either. For the first time in my life, I had a purpose. I felt confident and a reason for self-worth. Instead of the little girl with her faced pressed against the glass, looking out across a dreary neighborhood, with no purpose and no future, I had become someone determined. Every one of my mother's notes helped me become a young woman, strong with intention.

For I know the plans I have for you, plans to prosper you and not harm you.
Plans to give you hope and a future.
Jeremiah 29:11

Mom noticed something in me, and I noticed something in her. Maybe she saw a piece of herself in me, a life that she could never have. I certainly recognized a desire that had always lived inside of her. My whole life, Mom was screaming inside. I could see that now. And silently, we'd been screaming together all along. The more I matured, the more I came to understand her.

My evening routine didn't change much even once I was in high school. I came home from my track meet, took a bath, ate dinner, did my homework, and went to bed. Instead of eating with a table full of my sisters, now it was just me, Cheryl, and Damon. There were only two volumes in the house now—quiet or scary. While doing my math homework in the den, the telephone rang. I heard Dad pick up the phone and I assumed it was one of his friends.

"There's a phone call for you," I heard Dad growl in the doorway behind me. My back stiffened and I froze with confusion. Dad was steaming, his skin cherry red. It was a boy.

We weren't allowed to receive phone calls from boys. Dad wanted us for himself to use and abuse. I understood that now. But it was never hard for me to keep up with the rule because I never socialized with anyone. Until now. A boy on the track team took an interest in me and although I told him not to, he called. I got up from my homework and nervously looked at Dad. He was mad and had a smart smirk on his face. I could tell he thought I'd crossed him.

I picked up the phone and quietly said, "Hello?"

Dad stood at the kitchen entrance, staring at me, watching me talk on the phone, waiting for me to say something inappropriate. I didn't want to say anything at all. I could see Dad out of the corner of my eye, tapping his fingers against his crossed arms. His mouth was fidgeting with impatience so I quickly ended the call. It wasn't worth the showdown.

"How many times have I told you not to have any boys calling this house?" his voice rose as he spoke, yelling at me by the end of his sentence.

"Yes, sir," I said, my head still drooped. I was cowering in between the refrigerator and the stove, hoping he wouldn't come for me.

"What in the hell am I going to do with you?" he was getting even more frustrated.

I stood back in the cubby, waiting.

"Go ahead. Go into the other room," he relinquished and let down his arms. Dad turned like he was headed back out into the hallway and I followed. As I rounded the bend to go back to the den, Dad swung around and punched me in the stomach. All of my air shot out of my mouth, and with the last of it, I screamed. He caught me by surprise. Tricked me. Gotten revenge for my phone call.

I doubled over trying to catch my breath and fell to the ground. Mom came running into the kitchen followed by Cheryl and Damon. While I couldn't speak, Dad told them I tripped and then sauntered back to his room. I watched him walk away with disgust. He didn't even look back at me. I was roadkill to him.

Mom kneeled down to help me up. Softly, she whispered, "Is that what happened?"

I looked her in the face. My eyes were welling, "Yes," I cried, "I'm fine."

She didn't argue with me. She didn't push for a more truthful answer yet she had to know that I was lying. *How could she not?* I couldn't tell her the truth out loud. I couldn't tell her the truth about anything. I knew that if I were honest with her that the price for telling was too much. I knew it was best to be quiet.

Deep inside, I wanted to tell Mom. I wanted to confide in her and tell her everything that Dad had ever done to us. I wanted her to know, from my lips, exactly what had gone on for years under the roof of her house. I wanted her to hold me and say that she didn't know and that she didn't mean for any of it. I wasn't even looking for an apology. I wasn't looking for anything specific from her. I just wanted to pour it all out, to empty all of the pain pent up inside of me, and I wanted to empty it out to her. But I couldn't. Ever. I just rubbed my stomach, cinched over a little with the pain, and walked to my room to lay down. I didn't want her to see me cry anymore.

When Mom picked us up from school the next day, she drove us to McDonalds. I knew something was wrong. We never ate fast food. We hardly ever ate outside of the house. As Mom pulled into the parking lot, I looked over at Damon and Cheryl who wore expressions that were just as puzzled as mine. Mom was crying. As she shifted into park and shut the Travelall off, tears streamed down her face uncontrollably. She was crying harder than ever before.

"I'm sorry," she kept stuttering, her voice soaked and muffled. A long minute, one that stretched over a cascade of feelings inside of me, went by before Mom could bring herself to turn around and look at us. Her face was dripping. The three of us sat attentive, unsure if we should console her or what was going on.

"I'm tired," she let out her breath. "I've been tired for a long time. I never meant for you and your sisters to deal with all this," she searched hard for the right words. Confusion and befuddlement took over her face. "Your dad," she started, but trailed off, and was silent.

I watched her struggle, squirming to find the words. She felt convicted to make some sort of reconciliation here and I wasn't sure how to take it. I didn't know how to accept an apology, and more than that, I didn't really want her to apologize. I didn't want to blame her so I never had, and now, she was trying to give me license to do so. The conflict became less about her acknowledging what we'd been through and more about accepting that she had responsibility in it. She was giving us permission to hold her accountable by apologizing and that wasn't going to make it better for me. I needed my mother to be strong. I needed her to persevere like she always had, no matter how many apologies she thought she owed us now.

"We're going to stay with grandma again," she said more calmly. She'd already devised a plan. This was the first step of it.

I started to shake my head. I wanted her to stop what she was doing. Although I wanted more than anything to get away from Dad, I knew we could get through it because, relatively, there wasn't much time left before it was over. I was shaking my head in disbelief, but also to tell her, *No, don't say you're sorry. Not now.*

"Diana," Mom looked at me directly. "Is it true? Did your dad," she had to push the words out of her mouth, "Did your dad do something?"

I sat there, stunned, a deer in headlights. I knew what she meant. Cheryl and Damon were silent, staring back and forth at me and Mom. I didn't know what to say. *How did she find out?*

"Is it true?" she demanded with tears rolling down.

Meekly, "Yes," I responded.

I did it.

I told.

Everything would change now. Now it was real.

Mom looked at me with swelling anger. The disgust in her eyes battled with flashes of sympathy and guilt.

"Diana," she let out with her breath, "why didn't you tell me?"

In that moment, everything convalesced. My whole world exploded into a vast expanse of confusion again. I felt deeply embarrassed and couldn't look at Cheryl or Damon. I knew Cheryl knew but I'd never asked her to acknowledge it. I wondered about her too. Tears burned my cheeks. I was scared. I was vulnerable now and I didn't think that the outing of my deepest secret could lead anywhere but to some dark, even more terrifying reality. *What if she confronts him with this? What will I do then?*

"I'm sorry, Mom," I started rambling, "I just…I just didn't know what to say or how…" I couldn't get any of the words out because I didn't even know what I meant to say.

Everything is my fault. I should've done better. I shouldn't have let those things happen to me so that we wouldn't be here now, in this moment. I shouldn't have told her. I shouldn't have put this burden on Mom. I was so sorry that my father ever laid a hand on me. I was so sorry that I told Mom. I was so sorry for ruining things for everyone. Joni Jackson, my superwoman, had been broken. By me.

When we got to grandma's, I felt relieved. Mom assured us that we'd be there for some time so that she could sort things out. It felt like vacation and I needed the break from Dad. I needed the break to figure out where I was to go from here. Having my secret presently fresh in the world, out for people to know, I needed some time to be secluded and to figure out how I'd deal with all of this. Grandma's house was a safe haven.

As quickly as I put my bookbag down, I was picking it back up. Mom said that we had to go home to pick up some things before bed and that it would be a quick trip. I didn't understand. *Why can't we stay here while she goes to get everything? Why do we have to go back already? Even if it is only for a few minutes.* I thought that she was keeping me away from Dad now that she knew my secret. I thought that she had granted me reprieve. But I trusted what she said, that we'd be back to grandma's house before dark, and got into the car.

I don't know why I believed her. This wasn't the first time we left home nor was it the first time we quickly thereafter returned. Mom and Dad talked alone in their room for a long time while we waited in the den, looking at the ground, sulking. I looked out the window at Gladys' house. There was soft smoke pumping from her kitchen window. She was probably making dinner, fresh bread, bean soup, or cookies. I wanted to climb out of the window and escape to her house so badly. I would've taken Cheryl with me. She sat sulking too, coughing, and waiting.

"We'll just leave tomorrow morning," Mom came in. "Your dad and I have some things to discuss," her demeanor had changed. That cool, regal style returned and her upturned chin assured me that we weren't going to leave in the morning either. Dad had talked her into staying and we were going to be stuck again. We were back home to stay and I was so disappointed in her.

Days rolled on quietly. No one knew what to say.

After a week of awkward, but peaceful silence, Dad called me to the front room. It was alarming. I thought that maybe Mom's threat to leave this time convinced him to back off of us. I thought it might be over and hoped that my last two years in the house would be as quiet as the past week had been. I thought wrong.

"You need to stop trying to build a wedge in this family, Diana," he used heavy gestures to show me how serious he was. He'd been perseverating on this for days. "It's not going to work. Do you hear me?"

"Yes, sir."

There was nothing that happened that Dad didn't blame me for now. I think he hated me ever since I'd fought him off in the bedroom. Although he was always suspicious of all of us, his conspiracy theories became grander and solely centered on me as the mastermind. Ironic that the man who preyed upon me, who spent most of my life belittling me and whittling me down into a person who he could swallow up, now feared that I was trying to destroy him. Maybe I should have been. Maybe his fears weren't all that irrational after all. But I wasn't. I wanted nothing more than to whiteout every memory with my dad and to move on with my life, away from him, away from this house, away from this town, and away from my entire childhood.

Dad sat down and stared at me. His eyes pierced mine, but I wouldn't cower from him. I wouldn't look down like he wanted. I'm not a dog and I wasn't going to be intimidated anymore.

"Did you hear me?" he said again, slowly and sharply, as if I hadn't answered him before.

"YES. SIR," I responded with as much gusto as I could muster. I made sure he could hear me and I used my best military voice and posture to convey my attention, and to be smart. I would match his sternness, decibel by decibel, as I pierced into his eyes with mine.

Dad looked at me, shocked. His eyes widened with rage, and he smacked me across the mouth with his yellowed paw. His hand smelled like cigarette butts as it brushed across my face.

I whipped back to attention. For a moment, Dad didn't know what to do or how to react. He was tired. I could see it about him lately and I was bigger than I'd ever been. We'd been playing cat and mouse for so many years that I think a part of Dad wanted to relinquish control but was too scared to let go. I was ready to break him down.

"You're disgusting," he looked me up and down. "Get out of my sight."

I won. From that point on, I started to ignore Dad more while putting my whole heart into sports. He became less of a threat. He felt shrunken to me, smaller, less important, and not as scary. Everything became a little easier after that day. The pace of life seemed to steady and while he'd still try to give me a hard time once in a while, I was able to back him down and walk away with my head still up. I looked at him differently now. Day by day, I built a new strength. I was the conqueror now.

From that point on, Mom worked harder to be more involved in my life too. She left notes in my shoes more often, and she asked about track and basketball every time I saw her. She took an invested interest in me now. Maybe she was trying to make up for lost time, but it didn't matter. I took it, happily. When arguments between her and Dad broke out, she was quieter now. She just let him ramble on, would shake her head, and walk away. She didn't care anymore either. For once, she cared more about me.

I knew that Dad was sick. I watched his health decline over the years. I watched him suffer tremors and sweats, delusions and confusion, but it wasn't until now, until I had truly shifted the power dynamic between us, that I realized how weak he was. I knew he had a bad heart, but Dad was sick in his mind. He was disgusted with his life and lived in constant conflict, both loving and hating us in equal measure. I could see now how trapped he'd always felt, both positionally in life and within his own head. It was tormenting to be my father's child because my father was tormented. His pain seeped out from everywhere and onto all of us like an infection. Now that he was defeated, all he had left was this pain. No power. No control. Just pain. And in this weakness, I realized the battle we'd been fighting our whole lives was never in our favor. Dad's mental illness was too strong for any of us to have rationalized or reconciled. In his weakness now, it was consuming him. While it hurt me to watch him be tormented, it was also grossly satisfying to let him writhe in it.

I dreamt of running away my whole life and I knew that getting away with it was a real possibility now. I'd daydream about how I'd do it, where I'd go, what freedom would feel like, but in my heart, I felt tethered down. God wanted me to stay. After countless nights of quiet begging to God, He'd never taken the doubt from my heart about running away. To do it never felt fully right. Strangely, I often thought about my dad holding me safely under the willow tree. Whenever I wanted to run, this is where my mind went, and I had no idea what that meant.

As part of Mom's new found interest in me, she enrolled me in the Miss Teen of Ohio beauty pageant. I wasn't even sure what that meant other than Mom must've thought I was pretty. Or, she must think I'm not very pretty and this was where I'd learn to be more like a girl. I couldn't tell. It came as such a

Ultimately, I felt like a fool, but there were moments when I felt grateful that Mom would even consider me to be a part of this. Even though I was surrounded by plastic beauty queens with beehive hair and miniskirts, I was in a beauty pageant. My name was on the roster, and thinking about that made me feel pretty. I wasn't trying to win. I just wanted them to look at my face. Really look at me.

We spent all of our spare time with choreographers who taught us a skit we were to perform for all of the parents on Sunday evening. We practiced in a grand auditorium with stage lighting and moving curtains. The seats were wrapped in red velvet and there was a booth in the rafters that controlled a spotlight. I was enamored. All of the girls buzzed with excitement to get dolled up and sing for their parents. This number would be the final blowout performance of the weekend and ranked in importance just beneath the third place overall trophy. I knew my parents wouldn't be there, but I wanted to do well for the parents who were coming.

The place was packed wall-to-wall on Sunday. Cameras were flashing everywhere. All of the girls were greeting their parents and families and introducing them to other girl's families. The event was one giant mingling of responsible parents, and there I was, watching how they all acted, like aliens. The routine was hokey but I went through the motions exactly like they taught us while I watched parents in the audience point at their daughters and smile and take photographs.

We sang. *"One, singular sensation, every little step she takes."*

As I danced and sang in a choir of middle-class china dolls, I watched each parent gloat over their beautiful and talented daughters. I knew Mom meant for this weekend to be a retreat from home that might also offer a jolt to my self-esteem, but for once, I couldn't get back home quick enough. I wasn't this kind of girl and I never wanted to be.

As the band struck the last note of our ensemble, I fled out of the auditorium like Cinderella rushing from the ball, hiding that she is parentless and poor. As scheduled, Mom rolled around the corner and I hopped into the Travelall mid-turn.

"How was it? Did you have fun?" Mom was eager to hear about everything.

"Yes, I did. Thanks for letting me go," I flashed her a fake smile, hoping not to hurt her feelings. She didn't ask any more questions about it. She knew.

If the pageant taught me anything useful, it was that Mom saw more in me than I had ever given her credit for. She let me go that whole weekend by myself. Although it seemed right that she should be there, she was also pushing me out into the world where she knew I wanted to be. She was trying to give me opportunity and that brought me closer to her. Between the notes in my shoes, the pageant, and her encouragement, I connected with her more deeply. She was trying to make me into a woman the best she knew how.

In my senior year, I was always in the local paper for basketball and track. I was faster and stronger than ever. Mom started to cut out all of the newspaper clippings about me and collect them together. She even came to a few of my track meets. As I cut around the corner on the 400-yard dash at a meet in Ottawa Hills, I heard someone yell, "Run, black girl, run!" Mom was standing in the bleachers, the only dark woman in a crowd of sunburnt porcelain, jumping for me. Until that moment, I felt uneasy about this meet because it was in a rich suburb and I was the only face of color in the jurisdiction. But Mom made me feel powerful and when she yelled for me to run, I dashed the remaining meters with pride. I was unique. I was fast. I was the best runner there.

I started spending a lot more time with Mom. I'd help her do chores and run errands. I looked forward to it now. She was less severe now than she'd ever been and I was enjoying the opportunity to get to know her. The mystery was starting to unravel a bit and I wanted to be there to find out about her. I still didn't dare cross her, and she still kept tight reigns on all of us, but her rule had shifted from absent authoritarian to present and authoritative.

Every week, I'd help her take all of our clothes to the laundry mat. Today was especially awkward because I had to hide a hickey on my neck—the evidence of my first sexual encounter with a boy. Though my encounter was a brief and G-rated rendezvous under the bleachers after practice, a giant hickey was plastered on the left side of my neck. Feeling pretty after the pageant might have made me a little more forward than I expected. I walked with my head tilted to one side, like I had a crick in my neck. I knew it looked weird but I had to keep my head cocked. There was no chance I was going to reveal this hickey to Mom. She kept looking at me with raised eyebrows and pursed lips as I loaded laundry into the machines like a hunchback.

I looked at her reassuringly. "It's just stiff," I said, congenially, pointing to my neck. "Slept on it bad," I chuckled a little to see if she'd join in. She didn't.

I went back to sorting clothes into the machine as Mom kept glancing over at me, watching me struggle to keep my neck bent and handle the laundry at the same time.

"Did it hurt?" she turned away and asked, stuffing a towel into the washer.

I froze and stared blankly for a minute into the machine.

"What?" I stumbled. "You mean…," I pointed to where I had my neck folded down, "You mean when I woke up like this this morning? Oh, yeah," I shook my head, "it's sore."

I prayed I wasn't caught.

"No. I mean when he sucked on your neck so hard it caused that bruise. Or, is that dirt?"

She said it so casually that I didn't know what to do. I didn't know how to respond with my words or my expression. I didn't know whether to be scared or to be relieved. I just knew that those words had come out of Mom's mouth and were floating around me, waiting for a reply.

Mom rubbed her fingers across my neck, effectively debunking the dirt lie before I could tell it. I thought I'd faint. I was busted. But then, curiously, she just walked away and started switching the clothes into dryers.

"Here, get these and put 'em in there," she instructed me. I was waiting for her wrath, for lava to spew out of her mouth, and for us to have to grab up our clothes and get back in the car so she could send me to my room at home. But, no. She just stopped talking about it. She showed me that I couldn't hide it from her and I straightened up my neck and worked on getting the rest of the laundry done. I was gripped by her tactics. And by actual pain in my neck now from having feigned an injury for so long.

All of the kids at school had been talking about prom since February. Now that it was tonight, all the girls were blushing, telling each other about the details of their dresses, and the boys were coordinating rides and after parties. The hallways were plastered with decorations and filled with gossip. You could feel the buzz of excitement everywhere and all of our teachers gave us a little less homework knowing that everyone was quite distracted. I was more excited about graduating soon and to be leaving St. Wendelin, never to look back. While everyone else had been looking forward to this year because of prom, I'd been plotting for this year my whole life. Graduate. Leave Fostoria. Never think about any of it again. But, naturally, there was still a part of me

Wendelin. I was excited to be out with Michael on a private date of sorts, but I quickly realized that maybe we shouldn't have left the prom. That coming out here alone built an expectation that I wasn't sure I was ready to fulfill. I swallowed with regret.

Michael asked if he could kiss me and I agreed. I knew that this would lead to more, but I wanted to kiss him. I couldn't deny that. I didn't think it was right, especially after Mom had placed so much trust in me, but that hormonal adolescent side of me took over and it happened. I let go and we took things all the way. I felt so overwhelmed with fear and panic. I was convinced that something terrible was going to happen—that my dad would show up at any moment or that I was going to get pregnant, even just from Michael's kiss. A flurry of irrational worries invaded my mind. Panic set in. I had to get out of there right away. Michael was respectful of my wishes, backed off, and we left.

I felt terrible about what I'd done with Michael. I never told Mom because I didn't want to disappoint her. I just went back to Aunt Alice's house and thanked her for all that she'd done for me. Ultimately, Michael and I went our separate ways and never spoke of that day again. A part of me wanted to see him again and occasionally I did at sporting events. He was nice to me but I could tell that he wasn't interested in me anymore. I know we didn't mean to do those things on prom night. He was just curious. I was too.

On Sunday afternoon, Mom and I went home. As we pulled in, Mom turned back to me with wide eyes.

"Promise me, as long as you live, that you will never tell your dad what we did," she had her finger pointed me at me. *"Promise me."*

Of course, I promised her. With this experience, I grew even more in love with my mom. She had been supportive of me the past few years and encouraged me more than ever before. I might not have made it through high school well without that. I think that once I was old enough to show my potential, Mom realized that she had to nurture that potential. She wanted me to have a chance and to make up for the many years that she didn't provide the same strength for my sisters. She wanted me to get out and to find myself, my purpose, my happiness. She didn't have to tell me or hug me for me to know, to feel, that she was proud of the woman I was becoming. She was willing to take risks for me. She was my savior and I was her last little girl.

CHAPTER SIX

aunt alice's porch

I started to garner bigger recognition in Fostoria when the local Kiwanis Club featured me as part of their *Who's Who of American High School* series. The article highlighted me as an accomplished athlete with no doubt for a future. I felt a little differently. Mom didn't. She took it upon herself to call the only African-American paper in Ohio, *The Toledo Journal*, to tell them about her talented daughter—a minority athlete with unconquerable determination and the record of a professional. A week before graduation, I was featured in the Freemont, Fostoria, and Tiffin News as a young black female athlete who wouldn't be deterred by circumstance. So, with high school coming to a close and graduation creeping up, I felt like I was just bubbling on the brim of greatness. I could feel my dreams coming true already—a shiny sliver of reality had been cut open for them. I was so close.

Saturday morning. T-minus six days until graduation. I woke up to a lot of commotion going on downstairs. Mom had just come home from working the night shift and before she finished unpacking her things, I heard Dad yelling at her. My stomach knotted.

I crept over to the top of the stairs and slid down the wall to listen. Just then, there was a knock at the door. It was a policeman who said they'd gotten a call.

"Yeah, I called," Dad said with a stiff voice. I could imagine him with his hip swung out, pointing his finger. "She can't take them!"

"Who?" Mom retorted.

"The kids, Joan. You can't take the kids." He turned to the officer, "She can leave. Whatever." Back to Mom, "But you can't take them with you." Dad was on fire. He'd found out that Mom was planning to leave him today. That she'd mustered up the gull to pack her things and leave Dad properly. When she'd left before, Mom would leave Damon and take us with her, so Dad never cared. Besides, he knew she'd always come back, and having us all gone for a few days gave Dad the space to binge carefree. But this time was different. Mom wanted to leave for good and she wanted to take us all, but Dad would never let her take Damon away.

We were called to the porch where the policeman explained to us that our parents needed to separate for at least a little while. We were all asked to decide which parent we wanted to go with. The burden of choosing which parent to go with, right in from of them, was awkward. Of course, I was going to pick Mom, but I had to do it right in front of Dad. I sure wasn't going to stay quiet and risk the chance that we'd be made to stay with him while my mother was sent to leave alone.

"Mom," I spoke up. I looked at my dad out of the side of my eye as I shuffled toward Mom.

"Me too," Cheryl said lowly.

Damon looked over at Mom, and then to Dad. I could tell that he was torn. With a long face, disappointed and defeated, "I'll stay with Dad," Damon said. Immediately, the officer sent us to grab our belongings. If her heart was broken, she didn't say anything about it. Mom didn't try to fight for Damon.

Mom dropped me off at my aunt's house and then took Cheryl with her to stay at our grandmother's house. The moment they drove away, I sat down on the porch and basked in freedom. I was far away and by myself now. I was disconnected from Mom and Dad, from my entire family. The breeze was warm with the scent of fried fish wafting from the kitchen window. Everything was quiet and swaying. For a long time, as the sun set, I just smiled.

T-minus three days until graduation. As I walked to my grandmother's house to see Mom, I thought a lot about Damon and wondered if he was okay. I wasn't too concerned, though, because Dad would never hurt him, but I did wonder what Dad was telling him. I wondered if he was talking to Damon about us, or if he was too stoned to treat Damon right. The more I thought about it, the more I feared how things might unravel. Mom had never left Dad for this long. I was starting to become hopeful that we weren't ever going back, but that hope came with concern for Damon. He was stuck there with my dad, alone.

On my approach to Grandma's driveway, I saw my dad's car parked. My stomach knotted and I stopped in the gravel. *No.* I swallowed and moved to the grass. As I crept closer, I could see my dad sitting inside his car, crying. I had to blink and rub my eyes a few times. I shuffled closer to get a better angle. He was crying. I didn't know if he was on his way out or had just gotten there, but I hoped he was crying because Mom had just told him to leave. Ducking down, I went around to the front door.

As I came in, Dad knocked at the backdoor and asked my grandmother to speak to Mom. I cringed in the foyer corner. *No. Please, no.* I thought maybe after all of these days that my mom had built up the strength to stay away. She seemed like she'd found stronger resolve, or maybe I just wanted to believe that because I didn't want to go back. I didn't want to have to give up this gift. I just wanted to stay, even if Mom went back.

Unfortunately, things rarely change, as life had taught me thus far, and on the next morning, we drove home, sulking.

T-minus two days until graduation.

My sisters came home for my graduation, except Andrea and Toni. With all them in the house, full grown adults, especially Janelle with her new husband, Bruce, Dad stayed out of our way. Dad despised Bruce, but that wasn't a surprise. It didn't matter who Bruce was or which one of his daughters he was married to, Dad was going to hate him regardless. Janelle never expected otherwise. It was almost intense enough to classify it as a form of jealousy. Maybe it was that intense. But Dad was visibly irritated for the couple of days that Bruce was around. Too irritated to even be happy about most of his children being home and for his youngest daughter to graduate high school. At the time, I wasn't upset about it. I never expected anything different from him. He hadn't paid me any real attention in years. For me, it was better that Dad stayed in the background so I could simply enjoy my sisters. I soaked up their company for one last day before we were all adults and we were all gone to different places.

Graduation day. Checkpoint. I was so excited. My freedom had arrived. My father couldn't have been more indifferent and I couldn't have cared less. I walked across that stage with stars in my eyes. If no one clapped for me, it wouldn't matter. I did it. I graduated, and now all that was left was the countdown to my birthday. Then I'd be off to college.

After the ceremony, everyone embraced me. My sisters, Mom, and Bruce hugged me. Everyone was so happy. Just not Dad. My sisters were so happy that we all made it. I rode all the way home with a smile plastered across my face.

As I set my cap down and started to unzip my gown, Dad had his finger in my face before even getting through the door.

"How many times have I told you that you are *not* supposed to go near Bruce? How many?" he yelled. "You can't be trusted. You never listen! I am so sick of you, Diana."

I didn't know how to respond. Dad caught me off guard, and at this point, I was just starting to piece together what he was mad about. I opened my mouth to tell him I was sorry so that he might calm down.

"No. You're disgusting! You're not going anywhere tonight. Go to your room," Dad shot his fists down to his sides and stared at me, waiting for me to walk away.

He couldn't ruin anything for me. I wanted to go out, to go to parties and celebrate graduation, but if I couldn't, that would be okay too. Because no matter how much Dad berated me, held me back, or took things away, he couldn't take away my diploma. He couldn't take away my freedom. When I was a little girl, it seemed like I would never leave; that I'd always be trapped with him because adulthood was so far away I couldn't even conceive of it. But now, my freedom was close enough that I could taste it. I had lassoed my way out and was only pulling the day closer. Dad could send me to my room for now, but ultimately, we both knew, he couldn't stop me from leaving.

Settling on this, I looked away from Dad and turned to head upstairs.

"No, Diana," Mom stood up and bellowed. She turned to Dad, "No, you don't have the right! What has she ever done to deserve this? Why do you do this?" Mom's face had snapped into an assertiveness that I hadn't seen come over her for years. Her cold voice shot through my dad and he stood there, listening to her yell at him, stunned.

"You will not tell her what to do anymore," Mom flipped her hand around.

Mom turned to me again, lowering her voice, "Diana, go upstairs and pack an overnight bag."

I stared at her, looked at my shocked father's face, then back at her. We were all just standing there, staring at one another. I felt nauseous.

"Go on!" Mom shooed me upstairs.

My friend, Angie, was outside honking for me. I ran downstairs and past my parents. I couldn't look at either one.

Dad shot after me, "If you leave, never come back!"

Mom ran out and stopped me, "After the party, go to Aunt Alice's."

She gazed at me sternly. I didn't know what was happening and I was scared to leave her there. She gave me a look that assured me she knew best and that I didn't have a choice. I shook my head and got in the car.

Angie had the music and a smile on, her hair glistening in the sunlight. As we pulled away, I just stared straight forward and didn't look back. I felt tears well up behind my eyes and my throat tighten. With every mile we drove away, more and more tears started to rush down my cheeks, harder and harder.

Today was meant for celebration. Not this.

Angie turned the music off, "What's wrong?" She put her hand on my shoulder.

I couldn't talk. I couldn't tell her why I was crying. There were so many reasons. The confluence of it all, the destruction of my graduation day, the pettiness and the heartache—it all came rushing. And my mom. *Is Mom okay?* Angie did what she could. She told me that she was proud of us, that today was a good day, and that no matter what was wrong, we were going to go have fun. I nodded and I went with her to one party, walking through it like a zombie. In short time, I asked her to take me to my aunt's house. I told her that I didn't feel well.

As we drove up, I could see Mom sitting on the porch, rocking in Aunt Alice's chair. I thanked Angie and waved as she backed out before heading up the porch steps.

"Did you have fun?" Mom asked as I approached. She smiled at me briefly.

"It was okay," I said. There was a quiet pause filled only with the hum of evening cicadas.

"Are you alright?" I asked slowly, sitting down next to her.

Mom looked away from me and started to cry. She was trying to hold it in, to squint her face in such a way that she could keep the tears bottled, but with no success. Her eyes spilled over and soaked her cheeks. It was uncontrollable.

"All your life," she pushed out, "All your life has been trouble and turmoil. All of it. Your dad is sick." Mom's voice trembled with her words. "I should have left him years ago, I know. And I'm so sorry," her tears streamed harder now. "I'm so sorry for putting all of you through it. I wish I could take it all back. You all had to go through so much and I never meant for you to get hurt."

Mom stopped to catch her breath, "I just didn't know what to do. I didn't! I'm sorry." More calmly she said, "I love you, Diana. I love all of you." Turning to me, she looked over the tears flowing down my face now and assured me, "I'll never make you go back."

In that moment, I knew mom was telling the truth. This time, I could tell that. I could see that she was broken. That everything she held together for so many years, everything that she blocked out and hoped to get better, was assaulting her. I could feel her sorrow, her remorse, and that was enough for me. I sat there, crying next to her, holding her hand, and believing in a new way. I promised her that I'd take care of her, that I loved her, that life would be better this way. I knew that she was asking for forgiveness, that this was her way. There was nothing easy about how she felt and I couldn't be upset with her like maybe I should've been. It was too late to change any of it and I was too overwhelmed to grapple with that. As much as my dad abused his daughters, he abused my mom too.

It might have taken her all of these years to be able to do it, but on that night, she drew a line in the sand for me. And over the course of high school, she had done what she could to change the trajectory of my life, to keep me motivated, and I was grateful to her. I fed on her strength, and I accepted her apology, which I never needed to love her anyway.

We never went back after that day. Mom had finally broken us free. The only person left behind was Damon, and I could only imagine the many nights that my drugged up father would spew out his anger about Mom to my brother. I know he grew bitter roots toward Mom. But none of that was up to me and now that we were free, I pledged to take care of Mom. Right there on my Aunt Alice's porch. I never had to see Dad again.

Diana, five years old.

This is Easter. My mom made all our ponchos! Left to right: Toni, Andrea (holding Damon), Cheryl, Diana, Janelle, and Lola.

Diana's mother, Joni.
High school graduation photo.

This is my father and I. I was around nine years old in this photo. Dad never smiled and he always had his hat on. That's Lola to the right.

These dresses were made from Butterick patterns, perfectly sewn together by my mom. Simply neat, perfectly poised, and ready for church, we were taught to be elegant, graceful, and lady-like. Left to right: Diana, Cheryl, Lola, Janelle, Toni, Andrea, Mom. Notice Lola looking after me.

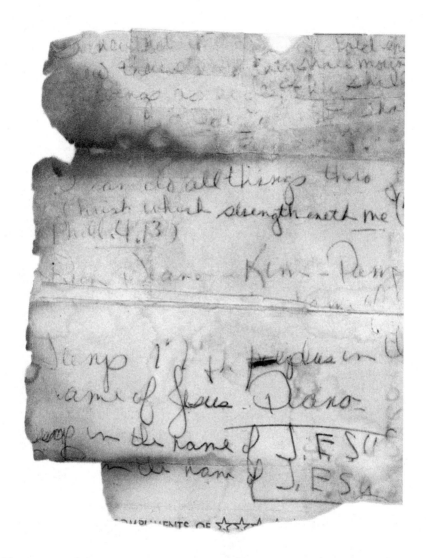

This is one of the notes Mom left in my shoes. In this one, she tells me to jump seventeen feet in the name of Jesus. These notes were written on the back of telephone bills or on paper towels.

Diana and her mother.

For brief moments like these, we were the perfect family. I loved Christmas, and Mom had put our pressed hair into rollers to prepare for the day. You can see the wicker cart behind us, next to the tree.
Left to right: Andrea, Toni, Cheryl, Diana, Lola, Janelle.

I went to Riley Elementary for a time because of desegregation bussing.
This is my class photo, 1979.

Diana, school photo.

Aristrocrats

The St. Wendelin Mohawks will crown a homecoming queen Saturday night in a game against North Baltimore. In the back row are the queen candidates. They are, from left, Pam Miller, Diana Pinskey and Lori Hoffbauer. Other members of the court are, front row, from left, Amy Hinrichs, freshman, Lisa Schumaker, junior, and Monica Weingates, sophomore. The queen will be crowned during half-time ceremonies and a dance will follow the game.

St. Wendelin homecoming court, 1986.

Pinskey, Lashuay to compete in pageant

Diana Rachelle Pinskey, daughter of Mr. and Mrs. Thomas R. Pinskey, Fostoria, and Beth Ann Lashuay, daughter of Mr. and Mrs. David Lashuay, Wayne, will be competing for the title of Miss Teen of Ohio in Delaware, Ohio, Aug. 2-4.

Miss Teen of Ohio will win an all-expense paid trip to the Miss Teen of America Pageant, a $1,000 cash scholarship and other awards, according to a news release.

The pageant utilizes six judging categories to find the most outstanding young women from around the country. These categories include scholastic record, service and achievement, personal development, poise and appearance, general awareness, and judges interview.

The pageant's official state charity is the American Cancer Society. The Miss Teen of Ohio candidates will be participating in a scavenger hunt to raise funds for the charity.

The charity events, the judging activities and production rehearsals will lead up to the pageant finals at Branch Rickey Arena on the Ohio Wesleyan University Campus Aug. 4 at 8:15

DIANA RACHELLE PINSKEY

BETH ANN LASHUAY

Miss Teen of Ohio competition. I did not win.

Left to right: Joey Anderson (cousin), Diana, Damon.

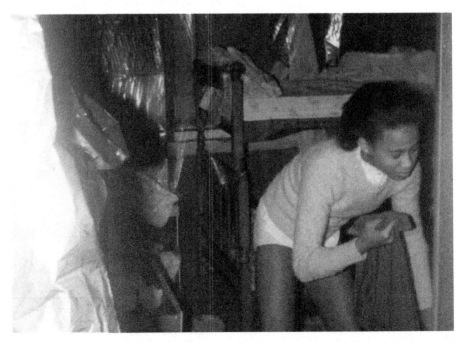

During my sophomore year, there was a fire in our house. This is me getting dressed in my room after that fire. I slept on the top bed.

Fremont, Fostoi

Diana Pinskey Chosen For "Who's Who"

By Michael Daniels

Diana poses here with her sister Cheryl (left) and mother Joni Pinskey (center).

Seventeen year old Diana Pinskey of Fostoria, Ohio has been chosen to be in "Who's Who of American High School Students," and no wonder. The St. Wendelin High School senior leads quite an active life, from running track, playing basketball to singing in the church choir. Diana is always busy. It's hard to imagine how she finds time to maintain her studies and her high grade point average, but she does.

Her mother, Mrs. Joni Pinskey says, "Diana is a very disciplined young lady, even with all her other activities, she still keeps her grades up so she can stay on the honor roll. Diana is willing to go the extra mile in order to reach her goals, and that makes me very proud. She takes books with her everywhere I really

Toledo Journal. June 5, 1986.

Diana, freshman year.

Diana at her grandmother's house during one of her parent's breakups.

(RT photo by Andy Duran)
Diana Pinskey tries for an inside hoop over H-L's Angie Mosier.

(RT photo by Andy Duran)
East's Diana Pinskey, of St. Wendelin, lets fly with a short jumper between West teammates Cara Risner (22) of Arcadia and Sarah Edelbrock (44) of Findlay.

Diana, senior year.
Fostoria Times Review.

Diana, senior year.
Fostoria Times Review.

Page 6   The Review Times, Fostoria, Ohio   Tuesday, January 28, 1986

Photo by Gina Haase

St. Wendelin's Diana Pinskey put up a short jumper as Lisa King preps for rebound if necessary.

Diana, senior year. Fostoria Times Review.

East stars

Pictured above are the boys and girls who will be representing the East All-Stars in Friday night's 14th Annual Boosters East-West All-Star Classic, which gets underway at Fostoria High School at 6:30 p.m. (girls) and 8:30 p.m. (boys). In the top photo are front, left to right, Aaron Smith, Frank Franco, Jim Reesman and Mark Ritzler. Standing, from left, are Dennis Herod, Jeff Crace, Tom Kuhn, Alec Cole and Coach Roger Holman. Kevin Curth was not present when photo was taken. The lower photo features front, from left, Corinne Schaefer, Amy Curtis, Phyllis Arbogast and Pam Brandt. S   ng, from left, Coach Mike Pressler, Amy Withrow, Diana Pinskey, Ann Strouse and Coach Mike L   red is Jo Ann Reardon.

East All-Stars photo, Diana pictured center.

Diana running high school track.

My beautiful mother. Mom is working on Andrea's posture,
holding her head up. Toni is to Mom's right, and
Janelle is in the foreground, taking off toward the camera.

Diana's mother, Joni Pinskey.

PART TWO

CHAPTER SEVEN

running from my life

I walked into the University of Toledo with nothing but the few dollars I'd earned from working at JC Penney and McDonalds over the summer while staying with Janelle and Bruce. Mom drove me to the top of the hill where my dorm was and asked if I wanted her to come in with me.

"Only if you want to," I said. I didn't have that many bags, but she insisted.

"Okay, I'll help with your bags and take you to registration."

"That's okay, Mom. I can carry them," I looked at her kindly, and grabbed a bag with each hand.

After settling my registration, I turned to Mom to say goodbye.

"Okay, Mom, I can handle it from here," I assured her.

She kissed me, gave me a big hug, and simply said, "I'll see you soon."

And that was it. There was no long, sad goodbye. No promises about how I'd be okay on my own or instructions on when to expect a care package. I knew Mom loved me. It was just time for the next chapter in my life.

I couldn't afford all of the books that I needed and I wasn't fully prepared, but it didn't matter. I walked in with a heart full of hope and a mind full of determination. I made it and I didn't plan on ever looking back. I was enamored by what college life had to offer me—a safe room, new people, parties, but most of all, freedom. True, uninhibited freedom. In this world, I could eat what I want, say what I want, dress how I want, and go to bed when I want. This was my entrance into the land of my dreams, into greatness, and I was determined to make this work no matter what I'd have to do.

I walked up to the seventh floor of Parks Tower and met my resident advisor who escorted me to my dorm room. I met my roommate, Javette. She was African-American, had a long Jheri curl, was reserved and somewhat shy, but very nice. Javette enjoyed playing her music late at night, painting her nails, making sure her hair looked good and that her clothes matched. I wasn't sure if she ever went to class because she was always in the room when I came home from class or practice. I never saw her study much. No matter when I went back to our dorm room, she was always there. She didn't like socializing or going to parties, but was constantly primping her hair and outfit. I saw her play cards a lot in the community room too. But that was about it.

I, on the other hand, was always on the go, always doing something, and running around like a crazy person. But not calm, cool Javette. She was interesting to me. She was also the first of my peers to treat me nicely. She was a relief from what I was used to in high school. I figured there were more people like her here. There just had to be.

Surprisingly, at first, I treated college much the same as I treated life at home. I was often home early, kept up with my work, and went to bed probably before most of my peers had even decided where they were going for the evening. I didn't do this on purpose but it came to me instinctually now, and was probably for the better. But I was always curious—watching people, walking up to people, introducing myself to see what kind of reaction I'd get, smiling, always exploring, without fear. I was always thinking about a plan. I was working, moving toward a goal, keeping focused on the future, never stopping to ask myself if I needed a break. *No, you're okay,* I always told myself that—I beat it into my brain.

In this world, I finally felt the freedom to truly socialize and allow myself to be the interesting person I always felt I might be. Everyone was into expressing themselves, but, in a way, I didn't really know what that meant for me. I didn't know how to evolve to fit in. Again, I felt in limbo, like I needed to choose again—black or white? This, too, came instinctually. I'm not sure I had a reason to feel this way anymore. It was just what I made up things to be.

I was on a mission in college and I didn't waste any time. Within the first few weeks, I went to the Student Union to learn about what organizations were available to me on campus. This is how I found the Black Student Union, which I quickly joined and became attached to. I found myself committed to all the aspects of campus life through the BSU—black sororities, dances, and interest groups. I was a part of it all. I found my place. Chose a side. I never even considered the white sororities or groups. I didn't naturally identify with them and never felt like I'd fit in there. But no matter how much I clung to one group, or to one ethnicity, or to one type of interest, the conflict inside of me never dissipated. I batted it away, shoved it down, chose to be fully black, but I couldn't erase the reality of my true identity.

Something happened when I finally left Fostoria, something that I wasn't even aware of. I'd spent a lifetime waiting for the day that I could run away from it all. I had spent so many nights crying, wondering when my freedom would come, when I would be big enough to strike down the chains that bound me, to leave my father. I had waited for so long and now that the time was here, I was finding out, very quickly, that it wasn't that easy—that

I couldn't just run away from it all. Like a parasite, the baggage left by my father clung on to my insides and traveled to college with me. Physically, I was all alone, but emotionally, I was tethered. I acted in ways that I never imagined I would, in ways that were to disgraceful to God, and no matter how embarrassed I felt, I couldn't stop.

I started to talk a lot. Like more than anyone should talk, and it became disruptive to my classmates. I couldn't stop the sentences from pouring out of my mouth. I couldn't stop trying to make stupid jokes, impress other people, or prove things to them. It was like being eight all over again, small and annoying in a sea of legs kicking me away. I just wanted the attention. I liked when I did something right and everyone paid attention to me so I figured that if I kept it up, every once in a while, one of my jokes would crack a smile, or some of my quippy knowledge might earn me a little respect. But it all backfired. I didn't know how to do it right. I didn't know how to get the right kind of attention, especially from men.

I wanted to be noticed unlike ever before. At home, I did everything I could to stay out of Dad's way. But now, in this expansive world of collegiate freedom where happiness seemed tangible and impulses went unchecked, I wanted someone to see me. I wanted to know that someone thought I was beautiful. I wanted to feel important—like I was a real person with interesting thoughts and a nice smile. Maybe that could be true now that I was outside of Fostoria. I had hope that it was and I couldn't help but seek it out.

I was too scared to join a sorority right away. Those girls had everything I wanted, but on the outside looking in, they were also everything I didn't want to be. For whatever reason, they reminded me of the pageant girls with bouncing hair, trying to fit into that perfect square, polished with sparkles and pom-poms. I just wasn't ready for that, maybe I never would be. Instead,

I found a small social group of thirteen girls in my class who were looking to connect with other people on campus. I thought we had a common goal.

Quickly, and unexpectedly, I felt dismissed by them. They scanned me pretentiously, like the ugly duckling of the group. It was St. Wendelin all over. There was no way that I could stuff myself into their mold. I'd never be like them and they knew that. I'd never look like them and they hated me for it. They were the people in Pioneer Mill. This was never going to go away.

For one of our introductory meetings, we were all asked to showcase a talent. Unless long jump or running a 400-yard dash counted, I didn't know how to do much of anything else. The only real talent I had was being able to sing, which I'd learned in the choir. So, I sang *Amazing Grace*, with my whole heart.

As I stood in the front of the room, my hands held together, belting out *Amazing Grace*, everyone just awkwardly stared at me. I didn't expect them to react that way. *Amazing Grace* was a song that I'd been singing my whole life, a song that reminded me of my blessings, even in the worst of times. So to feel the buzz of disapproval sweep through the room, to have a shiver of embarrassment creep up my back, broke my heart. I was sharing something inside of me with them through this performance, but they didn't care. A couple of girls even booed at me while others laughed. I sang the entire song anyway. I sang every verse until it was finished.

These people were nothing like me, and all the expectations I had for how different college life might be were shattered. I was still the odd one out. The persecuted. The insignificant one with black feelings that counted less with no knowledge of how to normally socialize. I stood for God. Now that I had accomplished leaving Fostoria, God, running, and grades were my focus. But these girls stood for nothing. Their vapid concerns and mindless conversations made no sense at all to me. They were shallow and directionless, yet I was the outcast.

"Are you from Canada or something?" I heard a voice say.

A tall, thick boy from a neighboring fraternity was staring down at me, watching me twirl the hem of my dress in my fingers while staring off. I'd left the party to come outside to think. I was debating leaving and quitting the group altogether.

I looked up at him, confused, "What?"

"It's just, you're not like everyone else. You're different," he struggled not to insult me.

I was different. Completely different.

"Is that a bad thing?" I asked him, sitting up straighter, and watching him notice.

"No, not at all."

I didn't even ask him his name before I was kissing his lips. Something came over me, something that I never felt before. I succumbed to the small bit of attention he went out of his way to pay me and I reveled in taking full advantage of him. He noticed me and that made me feel special. While everyone else turned their noses up at me, he looked at me on purpose— actually followed me outside to do so. I could see in the way he looked at me what he wanted, and even if it shouldn't have, it flattered me. It consumed me. I didn't make him prove anything to me before leaping into his bed. He was just a boy who looked at me and I gushed. He thought I was pretty and I was impressed.

No matter how big the divide between those other girls and me, there was one thing that I could control the same as they could. My body. It didn't matter as much as they thought it did that I wasn't the typical "type." Men wanted all of us. And I wanted to feel needed.

I felt dirty the next morning. I woke up feeling a filth that couldn't be washed off. As I sat up and stretched, I was immediately brought back down with burden. A sickness in my stomach curled me over. I didn't want to feel bad about the night before. I didn't think that I should have to, so I jumped up and went running to get away, to let my mind escape for a while.

With each breath, I tried to sort out what I was feeling. I told myself that I hadn't done anything wrong, but then, I also quietly apologized to God for my indiscretion. I couldn't settle on a certain way to feel, but I did remember how it felt when that boy looked at me. I remembered how it felt when he wrapped me up protectively, when he took me.

You're disgusting.

I snapped out of my thoughts about him and quickened my pace. I was spending too much time on this when I couldn't change it now. Instead of arguing with myself, I thought about the other girls in my class. I wondered if they, too, did what I did last night. I assumed they did. But it wasn't the sex that I enjoyed the most. I craved the thing that came with it. It was the attention. The one-on-one absolute focus that couldn't have been broken. Those moments in time are forever mine, written into history that for one night, I got to be special to someone else—unique and important.

I breathed in and smiled as the morning air filled my lungs. With that thought, that reassurance, I turned the corner back onto campus and headed to my dorm.

I decided that I couldn't hang out with this group anymore; that it wasn't a good fit for me. I had plans, goals, and ambitions, and with this group, I was quickly getting strung up into a dangerous web.

I needed to get some sort of work. Five months into college, I was running out of grant money and I used the little bit of cash I had to eat with. I knew I couldn't live off of credit cards, so I sought out career opportunities and consulted my track coach, Betsy Riccardi.

Coach said that I could come to practices and work with the girls on the team, but since she knew nothing about me, she could not give me any money. Besides, all of her money was committed to other athletes who earned their college scholarships. But that didn't stop me. I started showing up to practices early, running extra laps, working extremely hard, getting to know the other girls on the team, and I even asked if there was anything I could do around the athletic office to help out. I was desperate. I needed something to come through and I thought it could be track, so I continued to try and make an impression.

Fitting in wasn't easy. Some of the girls on the track team immediately took an attitude with me. They really didn't like Coach Betsy telling them what to do, so her taking me in didn't make them respect me at all. The other girls were always late for practice, always talking when the coach was trying to conduct the day's workout, and they always cut corners. Coach hated that. She'd always tell me, "Work hard no matter who is watching." By the end of the season, the coach had enough, and those girls were kicked off of the track team. As they were pushed out, I was welcomed in.

With a smile, the coach congratulated me, "Your work has paid off, Diana. Welcome to the track team as a scholarship athlete."

Coach was able to give me ¾ scholarship. This type of scholarship arrangement was great because it allowed me to focus on getting a job while being on the team. The following Saturday, I put on a suit and attended a career fair at the University of Toledo, Community and Technical College. Since I was enrolled in the Paralegal program, I thought I was ready to secure a part-time job in my field. I walked right up to the Owens-Illinois table and met a gentleman by the name of Dave Stratso. He asked me a lot of questions, and I was able to look him in the eye and answer all of them. He saw me. Dave recognized my determination. He could see that I wasn't a typical college kid—I was a motivated young woman. He offered me a part-time job on the spot. I couldn't believe it.

My plan was coming together. I secured a part-time job, a very good job, and received a scholarship to run track for the university. The only thing still missing was my longing and desire to be noticed by a man.

I kept searching for that moment again when someone would notice me. I took note from the other girls in my class and became almost entirely preoccupied with being pretty. I spent time perfecting my hair, brushing on makeup, and wearing girlier clothes. It all made me feel beautiful. It made me feel mysterious. I started to go to dance parties like never before which made me long for Thursday nights and weekends.

The right man was hard to find this way. Sure, a lot of guys paid me attention, but that attention was momentary and ended the minute I put my clothes back on. *Not the one*, I'd think. Deep down inside, I valued myself in a weird way—enough to keep up the search, I thought. I was willing to forgo the values that I thought I had just so that someone would look at me. I prayed that if I allowed these men in, they would see inside me, they would see my heart, and they'd care about me. One might even love me. But, in reality, I was subconsciously searching for something much, much deeper— trying to mend something inside of myself that was very broken. My drug was love and I was chasing the dragon. Every time a guy would hold my face and look at me before taking me back to his room, I thought that he was looking into me deeply, that he wanted to understand. And every time a guy would complement me, I felt like I needed to show him my gratitude for it.

No one ever taught me how to value my body. The only man that was ever close to me made me devalue myself. Dad had carved an internal impulse in my brain that triggered every time I met a man who gave me so much as an interesting look. My secret promiscuity started to bear heavy on my soul by the end of freshman year. I hadn't found anything that resembled love, and I hated myself for it. I was so ashamed, but even still, with each guy, I felt the hope of redemption somehow. *Maybe this one will be different.* I'd become so ugly on the inside that I couldn't even face myself. I couldn't sit longer in front of the mirror than I had to or I'd slip into a spiral of self-loathing and despair. I just kept going rather than face it. I kept it up hoping it would resolve itself. The year culminated so quickly into a single dark moment that I didn't quite know how I'd gotten there, and I certainly didn't know how to get myself out. I felt completely unloved by everyone, including myself.

You're disgusting.

I felt humiliated. Over and over. And I couldn't stop.

I was stuck and I was drowning.

You're disgusting.

I believed that now.

But I was smiling. I was the life of the party. I had the jokes. I was the funny one. Dancing. Trying to fit in.

This is what a breakdown looks like.

CHAPTER EIGHT

a time to kill,
a time to heal

Sophomore year opened with a glimmer of hope. I met my kindred spirit that year, Erica. We lived next door to each other at Parks Tower, and I knew the first time I introduced myself to her that our friendship would be magical.

Erica embodied everything that I always knew I was. I identified with her deeply—her vibe, her attitude, her persona, her *realness*. She was strong and smart with a dedicated work ethic that I admired. Finally, it felt like I was looking at someone who got it; who got me. When I looked at Erica, I saw a piece of my eight-year-old self. Seeking. Pushing. Wanting more.

While astute and focused, Erica liked to dance too. It wasn't long before we were driving to Michigan together, or dancing at campus parties. Erica quickly imprinted on me. She was meant to be my best friend.

As we got deeper into the semester, my schedule was wrought with track practice, work, and classes while Erica was focused on pledging for a sorority. We stayed as close as we could while maintaining our commitments, until I met Rodney.

Rodney was a football player who ran track too. I loved watching him. He wore big gold chains that I thought were so cool. Something attracted me to Rodney differently than the guys before. He was really nice to me. He paid attention to me without expecting anything to come of it. He looked at me because he liked looking at me. Rodney asked me out in the first month we met and from that evening on, we were always together. Like glue, we'd bonded together. I always wanted to be where he was. We embarked on a whirlwind of caresses and compliments, yearning and excitement. For everything that had ever brought me down, Rodney picked me back up only the way young love can. He bought me pretty necklaces and showered me with adoration. He looked at me the way I'd been searching for someone to look at me. It was first love. It was really happening.

Like so many people learned much younger than me, first love comes with the gravest of consequences. While most people find first love in their high school sweetheart, I was just learning what that high feels like, at twenty. Most people live through that devastating heartbreak that rips your soul up, leaving you to learn how to reassemble the pieces, before college. And because of it, most people are closer to knowing who they are by the time they go to college. I didn't know what was in store for us. I didn't even think about what was coming. I simply basked in a blissful place with Rodney. I never told him about my childhood or anything at all about my life. I didn't want to. I feared that it would taint what we had, feared it would taint how he saw me, and I couldn't risk it. It wasn't worth it. Besides, I didn't need that old life anymore. Rodney was my life now and with him, I felt stronger.

I learned that, no matter what, loving another person was always going to be a complicated issue for me. As infatuation faded and first love's veil parted, I found myself in love with someone that I really didn't like. A year had gone by and Rodney and I had moved past flattering each other and into a routine commitment.

We were living together.

And I was pregnant.

I knew it immediately. I was sick all of the time. I couldn't run a meter without getting nauseous. My breasts felt like they were swollen to my chin and a terrifying panic had taken over my body. I couldn't stop throwing up. Every time I ate, I felt like there was a chain being pulled in my stomach and flood gates being forced open. It was unbearable. And inconcealable. I didn't feel any flutter of excitement or happiness about the pregnancy. I didn't go to that place where new mothers start envisioning their future family in their new forever home, putting up baby gates. No. It felt like punishment, and I was puking enough that you might think I was possessed.

Rodney was worried about our careers. We were both lined up for successful futures in athletics and this would surely halt all of that. When I told him that I was pregnant, that I was absolutely sure I was, he looked at me hard.

"How are you going to take care of that?"

How am I going to take care of it?

He said it with such slick vagueness that it made it easy for him to argue that he supported whatever decision I were to make. But he also said it with such an inflection that clearly communicated what he wanted me to do. I ran to go puke.

On the weekend, we were scheduled to go visit Rodney's parents in Cleveland. They were a black family living in middle-class suburbia. I didn't understand it. The house was a modest ranch with a deck and a guest bedroom. I brushed my fingertips across the entrance hall wall and thought of Aunt Alice.

Rodney was an only child and his mother catered to his every whim. Whatever he wanted, things he didn't even ask for, she was there to bring him. It made me sick. Rodney could do no wrong by his parents and his total freedom had developed into a subtle cockiness that I started to abhor. Before this visit, I mistook it for confidence, but now I knew that I was wrong. It was arrogance. His whole life was a failsafe so he had no modesty.

They made a lot of BBQ meat for dinner. The smell of it made my stomach turn over and I had to choke back my nausea throughout the night so that Rodney's mom wouldn't catch on to our secret. She was offended that I didn't want to eat, but I couldn't. The thick, tangy smell of roasted pork slathered in BBQ sauce stuck to everything and everyone. I couldn't go anywhere that it hadn't invaded, and eventually, I snuck away to vomit in their bathroom.

Rodney was an athlete because he grew up with sports. Once they finished eating, he and his dad started right into a pickup game. Knowing that I was an athlete too, Rodney's parents encouraged me to play. I kept declining for fear that I might puke all over the court. I was green at this point.

"What's the matter, girl?" Rodney's mom looked at me, cockeyed. "Get out there and play!"

"No, thank you, ma'am," I smiled sheepishly at her, and then went back to staring at the ground. I was focusing on a singular point to keep my vomit stifled.

Rodney's parents must've thought I was so weird, that maybe I was disturbed, but I didn't care. Regardless of what they thought of me, the entire trip to Cleveland did little else than prove to me that I couldn't have this child with Rodney. I loved him, sure. But we had different values, very different perspectives on life, and I didn't think I'd survive six more months of seasickness. I opted to sleep on the couch alone, and couldn't wait to get back to Toledo in the morning.

Our appointment with Planned Parenthood was a week later. I laid in Rodney's lap in the waiting room, writhing with nausea. Sweat poured down my face as I waited to have an abortion. The decision to have it wasn't made with the utmost clarity. In situations like that, clarity is impossible. But the world seemed to be closing in on me more every day. Everything looked hazy in shades of green. Rooms felt smaller, my head always felt too big. Nothing about being pregnant felt right. It felt sick and cursed and my ability to tolerate it shrunk with every second. There wasn't a right thing to do. I just felt like I was doing what I had to.

The procedure was quick. In all, it took fifteen minutes to have an abortion and something about that felt weird; like it had been practiced. It was too easy. The nurse took me back to the room and smiled at me. I imagined she smiled like this at all of the girls who came in—like I'm crazy, but not. She smiled at me while suppressing her knee-jerk reactions, or maybe it was a sympathy smile. I'm not sure. I wanted to tell her about my life and explain that I'm not all that bad, but I knew she wasn't interested. She handed me my gown and showed me how to sit for when the doctor arrived. It was like going in for a pap smear. It was cold and I felt so alone. The doctor came in and introduced himself, but I didn't want to see him. I didn't want to look at his face or remember his name. I could see him just over the sheet that covered my legs when he started to work. No words. The whole entire time, there were no words. The nurse just kept looking at me. She held my hand with a crooked smile while I cried. I knew everything about this was wrong. I had to find a place to bury this away in my mind. Yet again, I had to find a way to bury something I was ashamed of and felt guilty for doing. I kept thinking, *Why? What am I doing here?*

I took a life. I took a life that was growing inside of me because I wanted to continue my career. I felt selfish and alone. I felt disgusting.

As I walked out into the waiting room, I also felt instantly cured. The nausea had completely disappeared, the room looked to be in normal proportion and color, and my body relaxed. It was gone. The torment was gone. But I couldn't simply wipe my hands of it and walk away unscathed. My body might've felt healed, but my mind felt shattered. I had to make what I had done right with God. I knew in my heart that He had already forgiven me because He knew the decision that I was going to make before I made it. I pled for forgiveness from God in the days leading up to this, but I still knew that what I'd done wasn't right and I had to figure out how I was going to forgive myself.

I was distraught for a long time. I couldn't do anything but battle remorse and guilt. I couldn't focus. I couldn't go out. I couldn't run. I was at a loss trying to figure out how to move on from it. Even if I settled my actions with myself, made it okay in my heart, I still felt guilty when I tried to stop thinking about. I felt like I deserved to have to think about it, to feel bad about it. Rodney didn't know how to console me because he wasn't conflicted like I was. He wasn't in it with me.

That spring, Rodney proposed. I don't quite remember it all. I think he felt bad for me. But I also think that since he was moving to Seattle for a new job that he wanted to tie me down. So, I accepted. I guess I wanted the security.

....

It was April, 1989.

Dad died of a massive heart attack. He was only fifty-one. Although he'd always been sick and he'd stressed his body for most of his life, his death came unexpectedly. He was alone when he died, in the front room, smoking cigarettes, looking at what was left of his life through the haze. I wondered what music might've been on, who Dad might've been listening to when his heart seized up, whose cries finally brought his final beat.

Damon hadn't graduated high school yet so he was the one who found Dad, cold and unmoving. I imagined the devastation wash over his face. His only friend was gone. And although the things that Dad taught Damon throughout his life may have been deranged and damaging, they had a bond that Dad never built with any of us. Damon loved Dad, and I could see the depth of the loss written all over Damon when I saw him. He sulked like he'd lost his best friend, like someone had stolen everything from him. He didn't say any of it out loud, but I could tell.

For us, Dad's death was a huge relief. There was an organic part of each of us that mourned him simply because he was our father, but the weight taken off of our backs in the wake of his passing was enormous, and the respite that came with it was bigger than my sadness. The end of Dad's time felt like the true beginning of my liberation. I cried briefly at his funeral in private, but then secretly hoped that his passing would bring me freedom. I hoped that the permanent erasure of his existence also meant the permanent erasure of my pain.

I was wrong.

It all happened so quickly. I arrived back home the next day and everyone was there. Though awkward, my sisters and I came together. I think we all felt confused. I didn't know whether to grieve, mourn, or to feel numb, but we didn't talk about it. We just worked to arrange the funeral.

That year, the song, *In the Living Years*, by Mike and the Mechanics came out. It was as if this song was made for us. It was an anthem to our father and it reverberated in all of our minds. We played that song at Dad's funeral. It was a unanimous decision.

From arranging to attending, Dad's funeral was a strange time. The memory of it whips from place to place in my mind. One minute, I remember sitting in Mom's kitchen, absorbing the idea that Dad had passed, and the next, I'm at the wake, dressed in black, solemn. Andrea sat in the back of the funeral home. She said nothing.

Mom asked all of us to line up beside Dad's casket. We kept his hat right beside his head because he never liked to be outside without it. One by one, each person came up to greet us as if we were animals at the zoo.

"Oh, you all are so beautiful. Look how you've grown."

Then, a lot of white people started coming up to us and Mom interceded.

"This is your Aunt Ann. Remember her?" Mom explained in a nice yet concerned voice.

Of course we don't remember her, they disowned us, I thought. As confused as I was to see them, I saw more white people come pouring through the doors. They were our aunts and cousins, but we'd never met them. When they talked to us, it felt forced. We struck up some small talk that quickly fell flat. There wasn't anything between us.

We had the funeral the next day. Once it was all over, Mom moved back into the house to take care of Damon and I could feel Damon's frustration emanate from his silent gestures. He shut down and closed us off. He was in pain and none of us could sympathize with him or console him properly. Dad always told Damon that when he died, Damon was to become the man, was to take over ownership of the house and his belongings, and to continue the Pinskey name. I think Damon took pride in those instructions, so when Mom moved back in, Damon began brewing an anger and resentment for both her and himself. Her presence there tarnished my father's wishes and Damon felt responsible for that. I should've stayed to tell him that Mom was doing the right thing, but I couldn't be there any longer than I had to be. My sisters and I were all gone as quickly as we had rolled in.

When senior year started, I felt just as burdened as I had all my life, only in different ways. Running away to college had not brought all the things I dreamed it would as a girl. While I looked happy on the outside, I was stricken with internal grief and confusion. *Where did I go wrong? Why did it all turn out this way?* College wasn't about freedom, or carefree living, or even academics like I dreamt it being about. Up to this point, my life had been riddled with heartache and confusion, disappointment and regret. Not much about that was different now. I had escaped my childhood torment only to replace it with an adult version. At the time, I didn't know what the word was for how I felt. The word I was looking for was depression.

Rodney graduated and moved to Seattle to accept his job offer. We agreed that I would stay to finish senior year and then move to Seattle too.

When Rodney left, things began to surface and people began to talk. There were rumors of other women and there was leftover evidence of it too. Getting a hold of Rodney became more difficult than it should've been. In my gut, I felt it. I knew what was happening. With a lot of suspicion and a little investigation, I found him out. Rodney had been cheating on me the whole time. A girl on the track team admitted that she and Rodney had been going out for a while. She lived in an apartment just doors away from where Rodney and I stayed.

I felt like I didn't deserve to have someone who was faithful. I felt like I had brought this on myself because I felt disgusting. Deep down, I still believed that.

Senior year was my best year in track. I was fueled by my frustration and the dismay that I felt toward a life that constantly evolved into new painful versions of itself. I ran hard like I had as a little girl, sprinting over train tracks. I took it all out on that turf. With that fierce expression of agility came recognition. I broke two records for triple jump that year in both indoor and outdoor track. I felt unstoppable.

The only thing that stopped me in my tracks was David.

Outside of track, I was always in the library. The track girls studied on one end of the library floor while the baseball boys studied on the other. I had a routine while at the library so I was jarred when one day, one of the girls leaned over to tell me that one of the baseball players thought I was cute. She said his name was David.

"Thanks, but all of the baseball guys are white," I quickly retorted.

"Yup, and David is too," she laughed.

I didn't quite know what to think of that, but I was interested. As I walked out of the library that day, I spotted David sitting at a study table with a few other guys. I gestured a quick wave and walked out, secretly thinking about how attractive he was.

The next day, I sat at a table alone in the library and hoped that he would come up to me. He did. After introducing ourselves, we found a quiet study room and talked until the library closed, until someone knocked on the door and told us we had to leave.

The next day, we did it again. We met in the library and talked for hours, seemingly unending. David had a calming nature that made me feel like everything was alright when I was around him. I was his focus. He liked spending time with me and I loved that. I felt an instant easiness with David and I was very open with him from the very beginning about who I was. I knew that he was sure of himself. He looked like he had a vision, a conviction in life. I could see it in his eyes and that was so attractive to me.

I knew instantly that David was special. I felt like I was in love the moment I saw him, but over time and after having opened up to him, I couldn't stop myself from clamming back up. I couldn't stop myself from receding back into my shell. I had to put up my shield of safety, my barrier of protection. I felt drawn to him so, naturally, I pushed him away. I pushed him away for a lot of reasons. One, he was white. I'd made a promise to myself a long time ago, when I was still a girl, that I'd never marry a white man. I would never have interracial children who would spend their lives questioning their identity and where they fit in the world. Being biracial had devastated me so many times over that I couldn't imagine continuing the cycle. To love David would have been selfish of me.

David didn't shy away despite my attempts to scare him off. We would sit and talk for hours about everything—something I had never done with Rodney. David didn't just like looking at me, he liked getting to know me. He was intrigued by who I was and that kind of attention, the kind I'd been struggling to find all of these years, scared me now. It was too deep, too penetrating. On the one hand, I held all of these secrets about my life that I was terrified to release. And on the other, David had a way of scooping out things about my personality, about who I was as a person, and exploring them. I didn't like it. The whole thing made me suspicious. *Why is he so interested in me?* If this is what true love felt like, I didn't understand why anyone wanted to let themselves get that entangled. *What is love anyway? How do you define it? Is love what I have with Rodney? Is it the thing that makes me feel inexplicably bound to him, no matter how bad things get? Is love what I feel for David? Is it this deeper, scarier thing that is threatening to out me?*

Yes.

Love was the thing I'd always wanted but never had. Love was a mystery to me. Now, within my reach, love was the thing that would put me in yet another bind. As soon as I realized that, I adopted a new mantra. *Don't leave yourself vulnerable.* I built up walls around myself until I was sitting alone in a very small room. I shut David out because I was wary about what new breed of heartache he had to offer. I finally met a man that wanted to treat me the way that I should be treated, in a way that I had never been treated before, and I ran from him.

But David ran after me. His perseverance was unrelenting and that made me feel singularly special. He listened to me. He sat with me while never checking the time. He wrote me so many love letters. He challenged me and made me reflect on who I was as a person. David's love, no matter how much I pushed it away, made me grow. I was falling in love with him and it didn't matter if I wanted to or not.

I spent senior year impressing on the track field and flirting with David. I took off the ring Rodney gave me but I didn't go so far as to totally break it off with him. I was torn between an obligation I felt to Rodney and the intense friendship and deep budding love I had for David. With graduation nearing, I had a decision to make.

I chose Rodney.

I felt obligated to Rodney for not leaving me after the abortion. I just didn't know how to *not* choose Rodney. After nearly two and a half years and all that we'd been through, I felt oddly committed to him, like we needed to see it through.

I told David in the school parking lot that I was moving to Seattle to be with Rodney. I cried through every word of that sentence. David cried too. Although he was disappointed, he didn't show it like he could've. David was gracious about it. He said that I should do what I felt was right and he wouldn't force me to love him. If I wanted to stay to be with David, then I should. And if I didn't want to, then I shouldn't. What a wonderfully terrible thing to say.

Besides David, who I could clearly see my future with, I gave up so much for Rodney. I was awarded a whole year of eligibility for track that I didn't take advantage of. I left it behind to go live with Rodney. Nothing could convince me that I shouldn't be with him even though I felt like I was doing all of the wrong things. Rodney had a piece of my life and I hated that.

When I got to Seattle, I tried to make the best of it. We lived in Bellevue, Washington just across the Puget Sound. I immediately started looking for a job and found a part-time position at a law firm downtown. I met some great people there. I took the rapid bus from Bellevue to Seattle every single day. It was so gorgeous out West. The weather was perfect. Seattle wrapped me up and made me feel happy. I never stayed in for lunch. I always walked downtown, taking in all of the sights. I loved the freedom that Seattle embodied. The city buzzed with creativity, was adorned with art, and served me up the best fish I've ever had.

I loved Seattle so much that I didn't allow myself to stay home very often. I stayed very busy and naturally, since I'd come here with shaky feelings about Rodney, we drifted apart. Rodney and I were two ships passing in the night. We never saw each other. He was always traveling for business and I was out working, gallivanting, and absorbing the city.

Truthfully, I was constantly thinking about David. In fact, there wasn't a day that went by that I didn't think of him. I even called him a couple of times while I was in Seattle, so it made sense for Rodney and me to drift apart.

I didn't mind the space because it gave me room for David. But David didn't understand why I was calling and quite frankly, neither did I. I just couldn't get him off my mind. I spent plenty of nights sobbing alone, wondering why I was doing this to myself. *Just leave*, I often thought.

A day came that finally pushed me out the door, a cosmic event that I couldn't ignore—the Universe telling me it was time to leave. I found some pictures in a Ziploc bag in Rodney's dresser drawer. It was of him with another girl. I squinted hard at the pictures, bore down on them and examined every pixel. The girl even had my clothes on. For me, that was it. *This is stupid. I need to go. WHY am I here?*

I confronted Rodney about the pictures as soon as he walked through the door. After stewing all day, I stormed up to him with them in my hand and accused him of what I had been suspicious of all these years. I didn't expect him to do anything except deny it. Even though this was red-handed evidence, I secretly hoped that he had an explanation that made sense. I wanted him to say something different than what I knew to be the truth.

"What is this, Rodney? And don't lie to me!"

Without hesitation, Rodney put his hands around my neck and lifted me off of the ground. I gasped in shock. His hands squeezed tightly, constricting like a boa, as I clawed at them. His face turned downward and Rodney looked at me with eyes full of hate. I hadn't seen him like this before. I'd also never caught him before.

I tried to push words out and to beg for him to let me go, but it was too late. Rodney had overpowered me, flopping my body onto the kitchen counter like a ragdoll, and then smashing my head through a cabinet. The room around me melted away and I was a little girl again, looking at my father. *No. STOP!* I was pushing his hands away from my legs and lunging my body toward the door to escape. *I am stronger than this.* I was stronger than Dad. No one could hurt me this way. Not Dad. Not Rodney. My arms wailed around and I opened my eyes as Rodney pushed me away.

I ran to the phone and dialed the only friend I had in the area, Christine. I could see Rodney huffing and pacing in my peripheral vision and knew that I had limited time. When she answered the phone, I spewed out that I needed help as quickly as I could. Rodney was over me before I could finish my sentence and ripped the phone out of the wall jack. I made a dash for the door but Rodney was just as fast. I ducked as he leapt around me and blockaded the door.

"You're not going anywhere," he fumed.

I stood there crying, rubbing the back of my head, trying to bargain with Rodney. He wouldn't budge. I felt delirious and everything around me looked lucid and floating. Nothing was standing still. Nothing made sense.

A knock on the door.

"Diana?" I heard Christine call into the apartment from outside the door. Rodney shot a dark look at me before unlocking the deadbolt. He kept the chain lock intact and only opened the door as far as it would allow.

"Diana can't talk right now," Rodney said, peering out at Christine.

I screamed in the background so that Christine could hear me. I wouldn't stop. I wasn't going to stop yelling so that Christine wouldn't leave without me. I would not be held hostage. Rodney turned and started yelling back at me that this was my fault, that I was causing the problem. I couldn't let him spin this. I wasn't interested in hashing out right and wrong, just leaving.

"Open the door, Rodney," Christine demanded.

Rodney got quiet for a minute, looked back at me once more, and then removed the chain lock and opened the door. I ran straight past him, into the hallway, and into Christine. We left as quickly as we could before Rodney changed his mind.

I was hysterical. I couldn't understand anything besides the fact that Rodney's rage confirmed his guilt. It was all a farce anyway. I was heartbroken. I left everything for Rodney. I left every opportunity behind to move to Seattle. I left David. Now, all I had to show for it was a smashed up cabinet and bruises on my neck.

I called my sister, Toni, in Orlando. I needed her. Toni wired me $795 for a flight to Orlando the next day and booked me a room at the La Quinta Inn for the night. She told me to stay calm, that everything was going to be fine, and that I'd be far away with her soon.

I had Christine drop me off at the La Quinta.

"Should I stay? I can stay with you if you want," she offered.

I told her that I didn't need her to, that I'd be fine. I asked her for a ride to pick up my things in the morning and to the airport. I really just wanted to be alone. I needed time to sort this out.

I slipped into a bath and gently washed the cuts and bruises on my head, neck, and hands. I felt sore and lonely. The whole day was like a car wreck that I couldn't stop replaying in my head. Every time I settled back and closed my eyes, Rodney's swollen, angry face invaded my mind. The breathless feeling of his hands wrapped around my neck. The sound of the wood cabinet crushing and splintering behind my head. I cried in the bathtub. I cried and smacked the water as a rush of desperation ran through my whole body. I wanted to scream it all out. Scream to God. *Help me!* I prayed.

I was exhausted from it all and as I got ready to crawl into bed, there was a knock at the door. I walked up to the door slowly. No one but Toni and Christine knew I was here. As I approached, a familiar voice came.

"Diana, it's me."

Rodney. *How did he find me?*

"Can we talk?"

"No," I said, and held my ear to the door.

"C'mon, Diana. I'm sorry. I just want to talk," I could hear him shuffling around. "Please?"

I opened the door and stood in front of him, not fully letting him in.

"Can I come in?" Rodney looked up at me with sorrowful eyes.

"No."

Rodney went on to beg me to stay. He said that he loved me and he didn't know what had come over him. He made a lot of different excuses, but quickly, his words turned to mushy sounds in my ears. I didn't want to hear anything he had to say. I was done. It was over.

When I got to Rodney's apartment the next day, all of my things were thrown on the curb outside. I packed them up and went straight to the airport. Everything was over. Everything was shattered with no chance of being put back together.

I cried the entire plane ride to Orlando. It felt like everyone was watching me sob.

Toni was at the gate waiting for me and took me up in her arms. I was so relieved to be held by her. She pulled away, looked at my soaked face, and told me that I may not *ever* mention Rodney again. Not once. That part of my life was over now. I nodded in agreement, sucked up my tears, and we headed to her house.

I stayed with Toni for about a year. The retreat to Orlando was like pushing the reset button on my life. In my last moments in Seattle, I didn't think that I would survive. I was so beaten down and discouraged and it seemed like there was no way back to the life I had always dreamt of having. I was lost then, but Toni gave me a space where I could find my way again. I knew I had to go to law school and that I needed to finish what I started. I started studying for the LSAT while dabbling in modeling on the side. I was surprised how naturally I fit into the modeling world. I secured myself an agent and worked prolifically in both commercials and print. Simultaneously, I got a part-time job with a local law firm and was back to running regularly. After a few weeks, I made a better recovery than I would've ever thought possible. Of course, my mind was still reeling about things and trying to work out the pain Rodney left in my heart, but I had hope again. I had determination again. As deeply as I had been stricken down this time, I rose up with more power than I had before. There was just one thing left on my mind.

David.

David had always been on my mind through it all. I never stopped regretting leaving him in Toledo, especially now. It seemed that the entire time I was in Seattle, I daydreamed about how it all might have turned out with David. Now though, I didn't know how he would respond if I called him. Almost a year had gone by and I didn't want to assume that he hadn't moved on in his own life. I didn't want to intrude. But I did want to intrude. I wanted to hear his voice. I wanted to see him again. I felt I needed him in my life. I called him.

David came to visit me. He welcomed me back into his life without hesitation. Actually, he visited me in Florida several times. I just didn't want to go back to Toledo with him because I wanted some time to settle, time to find a new way for myself before jumping right back into his arms. Although we knew everything was right, that I loved him and he loved me, I needed to sort it all out for myself first.

On the last Wednesday of the month, I was sitting in the breakroom of the firm, having my lunch, when I saw Toni's husband on the television. A breaking news story flashed onto the screen and when I looked up, there he was, being handcuffed and shoved into a police car, his corvette parked next to the scene. He'd just dropped me off in that same corvette earlier. The headline read, FBI DRUG BUST. My mouth hung open.

I immediately called Toni to make sure she was alright. She was crying on the phone and shuffling through things, trying to figure out a plan. I left work early and caught a ride home with a coworker. Subsequently, I was quickly fired from the firm.

This was it. Toni had been my confidant, and now her life was shattering in front of me. I called David.

David kept telling me to go back to Toledo and that he missed me, but I felt like I should stay to help Toni. She had swooped me up and taken care of me in my time of need, and now, I had the opportunity to return the favor. At the same time, my heart was pulling me toward David. I wanted to see him. I was dying to see him. Now that I had recovered enough to see the right path, I knew that path began in Toledo, with David. And that's what I told Toni.

I told her that I needed this time to completely work things out for myself, to fully finish my recovery, and to begin law school. She didn't argue with me. She knew that was the best path for me. And I left her. I left her when she needed me the most. I got on a Greyhound bus with a one-way ticket and promised Toni that I would make it up to her somehow, someday. And then I abandoned her. I still feel bad now for having left her.

Toni, Janelle, and Lola were the sisters who helped and supported me my whole life. They were the ones I turned to and the ones that I trusted the most. Yet, I had gotten myself so entangled in a revolving door of problems that I couldn't be there for Toni now. I just couldn't stay and I promised her that, this time, I would make my life work. I was really going to do it now. I owed that to her. I was committed to make what Toni had done for me worth her trouble.

Two people are better off than one, for they can help each other succeed. If one person falls, the other can reach out and help. But someone who falls alone is in real trouble. Likewise, two people lying close together can keep each other warm. But how can one be warm alone? A person standing alone can be attacked and defeated, but two can stand back-to-back and conquer. Three are even better, for a triple-braided cord is not easily broken.

Ecclesiastes 4:9-12

CHAPTER NINE

the beginning
of the end

My first year of law school started like any other year of my life—with a hurdle.

It was especially harsh that January. The blizzard of '93 was still passing through on its tail end, and walking to class was made difficult by piercing icy winds and thick snow piled up to my shins in some places. The world, inside and outside of me, was a cold, new landscape where I chose to navigate now with better caution. I was taking more careful steps, making more calculated decisions, sticking closer to my studies, and just trying to keep my life tame and controllable. I was building a blockade, a fortress of security, so that all the mistakes I made in college could never repeat themselves.

I sat in contracts class trying to be as astute as I could, trying to keep my mind from wandering around in the dusty corners of my memories. It had become even more difficult to stay in the moment these days. As I fidgeted to gain control, someone gently knocked on the door and pointed for the professor's attention.

"May I speak to Ms. Pinskey, please?" the woman pointed at me.

I gathered my books and moved to the door as a knot wrenched itself in my stomach.

"I'm sorry to interrupt you, but it's an emergency," she said, angling me to the side of the hallway. "Your sister called the school office and asked for you to call home right away."

"Oh, okay," I nodded at her. "Thank you," I said, and took off down the hallway.

As I trotted down the hallway, balancing my books in my hands, the first thing I thought about was Mom. *Is Mom okay? Is she alive?* I don't know why I wondered if she'd died, but I couldn't shake the fear of it. The last time I'd gotten a call like this, my father had collapsed from heart failure so, for me, it was commonplace to assume the worst. I quickened my pace and jogged to the payphone. Slamming all of my things down, I fumbled to insert a quarter and dial home.

Cheryl answered the house phone.

"Diana," she said with a frantic voice. "Can you come home right now?"

"Why?" I spun around, waiting for her to answer.

Cheryl tripped over her words for a minute, obviously trying to choose the best thing to say.

"Damon's in jail," she said simply.

It took a moment for that to register. *My sweet, quiet brother is in jail? No, not Damon.* Without any context, I didn't know how to react. I didn't understand. So I started asking as many questions as came to mind.

"What happened? Where is he? Why?" I started, took a break, and continued, "What?"

The class bell rang and the corridor filled with students. People were passing by me in every direction and the hall echoed loudly with commotion. I couldn't hear Cheryl anymore. Her words were muffled under everything.

"Cheryl," I said louder, "just tell me what happened."

There was a pause, and then Cheryl sighed, "Damon tried to kill Mom."

I stiffened up and gasped. *What does that mean? Tried.* I started to pick up my things as I yelled into the phone for more answers.

"What do you mean he *'tried to kill Mom?'* Is she alright? Cheryl," I was getting frustrated. There were so many people bustling around me. "Are you being serious?"

Cheryl just kept shushing me and telling me to calm down, that it was useless to talk about it right now, and that I should just come home.

"Mom's fine, Diana. Okay? Just come home."

"I'm coming," I said and took the phone off my ear. I stood there, just holding the phone, until the corridor cleared and I was alone again.

Quietly, I hung up the phone and swallowed the knot in my throat. I still couldn't understand what happened and was forced to run a million terrifying scenarios through my head. I was so confused that I didn't know whether to worry more for Mom or Damon. And if he had truly tried to *kill* her, what do we do now? *What has happened to him since I've been gone?* Flashes of Dad filled my head—blowing smoke and talking to Damon, laughing and jabbing at him to join, holding him at his side like a puppet. Now, in the aftermath of Dad's death, Damon had superseded him, and that made me so angry and so desperately sad all at once. Moving pictures of Damon being raised by a monster flooded my mind in painful chronology. Dad set Damon up for this. Groomed him for vengeance.

I walked straight to my car and got in. The road was thick with ice and snow, but I continued to buckle my seatbelt and heat up the car. I was cold from the outside air, but more than that, I was numb. I sat there while the car defrosted, staring into the sky. I wanted to see Dad. I thought that maybe if I concentrated hard enough, he would appear to me right now. I couldn't bear to think that we'd again have to live out my father's wrath through the likes of my brother, and I needed Dad to come to me now. I needed to tell him to fix it! To ask him, *Why? Why did you do all of these things? Why did you have to pollute Damon's mind?* He owed us answers and I wanted them now, here in this cold car, in this icy parking lot. I begged for him to face me in this moment.

I let my breath out, the cold air visibly escaping my mouth, and pulled out of the parking lot.

I drove home in silence. The quiet sound of the heat humming from the vents, the engine cranking down the road, and my busy mind were my only accompaniments. I had a small, irrational bit of hope left that I might hear my father's voice answer me. And if he had nothing to say, then maybe God would. I wanted someone to start talking. I needed answers and some instruction on how I was supposed to navigate this situation, this life of mine. I longed for His voice that night. I listened intently, waiting. But nothing came.

When I pulled up to the house, I couldn't get out of the car. I looked at my childhood home—over the bowing roof, the screened in porch, the cracked windows, over the street where I'd watched the neighbor kids, over to Gladys' house. A jolt of anxiety shot through me. I thought about Dad. I thought about how he wasn't here anymore. I cried about it all.

When I opened the front door, the familiar smell of the house, wall paint and a flowery musk, hit me and rushed over my senses. The smell wasn't as stale as it used to be. It wasn't mixed with smoke or anger anymore, but in it did linger memories that I wished I could forget. No matter how faint, the smell of this house, its eternal scent, will always greet me as a memento of unspoken tragedies. Mom was in the front room, crying.

"Mom," I rushed to her, "are you okay?"

Cheryl was rubbing her arm, handing her tissues.

"No, I'm not okay," Mom cried. "My baby boy! Oh, Jesus, my baby boy."

I began to cry as mom wailed for Damon. It was hard to stay in the moment and easy to keep crying. I couldn't help but drift in and out of past memories. My mind took me to terrifying places in this front room, put smoke in front of my face and then cleared it away. I looked at my mother, sitting there, in so much pain, head down and crying. She was so different now. The cavalier woman I once wondered about, the mystery woman, stiff with robust confidence, now sat in front of me withered and crying. Now that Dad was gone, Mom had shrunk down into a normal person. She didn't have to be superwoman anymore. She was still beautiful and cool and casually stunning, but she was softer now. It was surreal.

I wondered if Mom had called upon Dad today the same way that I did. I imagined that her resentment trumped her fear and that she would've been screaming out for answers. That she, too, blamed Dad for having primed Damon to do this. It wasn't fair and now there was no way to exact revenge, to make it right, other than to destroy Dad's legacy by helping Damon.

Mom just kept weeping and asking, "Why?" As we calmed her down, dried our tears, and found strength for her, she quieted and rocked back and forth before starting to recount what happened.

"I think he was possessed," Mom looked up at me now, her face shining wet.

"Tell us what happened, Mom."

For some time, Damon seemed transformed. He started wearing only black, he communicated less, and he was absorbed by loud music that got heavier and heavier. Damon seemed to retreat inside of himself, into a dark place where he wouldn't let Mom into. I don't think Damon ever really recovered from Dad's death, and now, having been governed by Mom these past few years, the person Dad probably taught him was the biggest enemy, everything converged into a confusing and dangerous place in his mind. Damon never had to be in touch with any of us. He never cultivated a healthy understanding of anything in the world. His universe was built in the front room with Dad so it should've come as no surprise to us when Damon imploded after Dad died. The internalization that your whole reality is shaped by someone with such demented intentions would drive any person spiraling into darkness and disparity. At best, I don't think Damon even really had the head space to cognize all of these things, rather just felt them very deeply.

Earlier in the day, when she'd come home, Mom yelled for Damon, "Damon, are you home?"

His abrupt and rude answer caught her off guard, "Yeah. Why do you want to know?"

Mom stopped in thought for a moment, "I just thought that was so odd, ya know?" I rubbed her hand to reassure her.

She said that Damon's voice didn't sound right and that she felt an eeriness. An alarm inside her head was going off. Something wasn't right.

"Mom, come here. I have something to show you," Damon shouted down the steps. Her nerves grew more anxious with this, her muscles tightened. The timbre in his voice was different.

As Mom set her things down, Damon kept calling her to go upstairs. In any normal circumstance, Damon maintained his distance, so his urgency for her to come to him made her worry.

"What is it, Damon? Just bring it here," Mom yelled back.

"No," Damon replied with a quick sternness, "it's best if you come up here."

Mom said this instantly made her feel sick. That her stomach knotted up with apprehension. I knew exactly the feeling.

Slowly, Mom crept up the steps, trying to peer around the corner to see where Damon was.

"Damon?" Mom called out, "Did you clean up here for me?"

But he didn't answer.

As Mom stepped up to the top step, Damon flashed over from around the corner and pushed her. He cranked his arms back and pushed Mom as hard as he could. His eyes glared at her, his face distorted, covered in sweat. Mom fell backwards, but as she did, she caught the railing halfway down. Clinging on to it, she guided herself and fell lightly to the bottom of the staircase. She stared up at Damon as he looked down at her. Mom laid there, paralyzed with fear.

"Oh, shit, it didn't work," he said.

Damon came running swiftly down the steps, beating each one loudly with his feet. Pushing herself up and backward, Mom ran into her bedroom and barricaded herself behind the French doors. Just as she closed the door, she saw Damon run past the bedroom and into the kitchen. As she picked up the phone, Mom heard Damon creeping around outside the door. He was wielding a knife and muttering for her to come out. As Mom dialed 911, Damon broke the glass in the door and stuck his arm through to try and open the door.

In the midst of her horror, Mom began to scream at Damon. She began to scream for God's help, to pray. Damon came at Mom like a tornado, setting down with lethal force, without provocation.

"In the name of Jesus, I rebuke you!" Mom yelled.

As the storm came to a thunderous close, Damon abruptly dropped the knife, ran upstairs, and slammed his door. Mom paused to listen. When she was sure that he was in his room, Mom ran to Gladys' house.

When the police showed up, my brother came downstairs just as meek and gentle as he always was and submissively put his hands behind his back to be cuffed. They led him into the police car without a struggle. Damon looked over at Mom with a long face of sorrow. He looked normal to her again, and when he lowered his head in pitiful remorse, Mom felt badly about it. She knew he hadn't meant to do this.

That's when Mom stopped and looked at me and Cheryl. She stopped crying, straightened up, and wiped her tears away.

"We've got to go help Damon," she said. "First thing tomorrow, we have to get to the jail and help him," Mom looked at each of us, and we nodded in agreement.

Mom never blamed Damon. None of us did. In that moment, we were banded together by our love for Damon and our hatred for what Dad had done to him. Mom wasn't looking for any explanation or apology from my brother because there was nothing to forgive. She just wanted to show him the love he needed and to help him pick up the pieces right where they fell. Mom wanted to show Damon her devotion, show him that she wouldn't condemn or punish him—she'd only love him. In her way, that was how she acknowledged the pain that brought him to this place. She could never change the past and she made it clear that her intention was to, instead, battle Damon's pain forward. Perhaps she was the one seeking forgiveness.

None of us got very much sleep that night thinking about Damon in jail, all by himself. I knew he was scared, and I couldn't help but flash back to that defenseless, gentle boy being pushed around on the playground. I felt the same way now that I felt sitting in the classroom, watching Damon be tormented. Helpless. More than that, lying in bed at night in this house again was torture. There were ghosts here and I was haunted by all of the secrets kept in these walls. It wasn't as easy as it used to be to escape into the dark abyss of my ceiling. When I looked at it now, I just saw cracked paint. The reality of it all was inescapable. Dad lived through Damon. I decided that night that rather than run, rather than turn away and cover my eyes until it was all over, I was going to save Damon. I knew I was meant to. My brother needed me and I was done running away.

Mom was clearly exhausted in the morning. She'd slept less than I had. The car ride to the jail was short and silent. No one knew what to expect. We pulled into the parking lot underneath the ominous loom of the county jail building. A stark overcast sat heavy on top of the jail turrets and everything was grey. It was cold and gusting and it felt like the sadness here could eat up a weaker person.

The hallway to visitation felt like a mile-long walk. Walking through the county jail, on our way to see my brother, took me out of real time. Everything slowed, blurred a little around the edges. The floor was grey with red and purple speckles—an odd choice, I thought, to have red dots littering the jailhouse floor tile. The orange brick walls felt narrow and smelled like a damp, musty basement. Honestly, I was scared. Walking down this corridor felt like another dimension.

Damon was being held on assault charges pressed by the police so we had to visit with him behind glass. We took our seats and waited for the guard to bring him in. When Damon came through the door, he walked like he usually did—shoulders drooped with his face slightly cocked to the side. He was dripping with sadness.

As I watched the guard unshackle Damon, all I could think about was apologizing to him. I wanted to tell him how sorry I was for ignoring him growing up, for resenting him. I wanted to say that I knew he could feel my bitterness all those years and that I made him feel unwanted. I was so sorry. It was never his fault. He looked so lost now, chained up in jail, confused and accused. *How did we get here?* Mom felt guilty too. I could see it all over her face. We had left Damon in the wolf's den, we offered him up in the fight, never thinking about the consequences he'd face for our mistake.

Mom broke down into tears again.

She peered at Damon through the glass, "Are you alright?"

Damon stared for a moment. His face started to contort as he choked back his feelings. He opened and closed his mouth, lost.

After a deep breath, he shouted to her, "Mom! I am so sorry. I didn't mean to hurt you." Damon was shaking his head and his whole body tremored with remorse. He didn't mean to do what he'd done.

"I know," Mom began to dismiss what he was saying. "I know, Damon."

"No," Damon pushed to say what he felt like he had to say, "I hate myself, Mom!" Tears began pouring down his face, "What did I do? I don't deserve you, Mom. I don't deserve to live!" Damon sobbed and repeated his apologies through a muffled mouth.

He was desperate and my heart bled for him. He had lost control over himself, snapped into the part of his brain programmed to defile us, programmed by my father. But Damon wasn't truly the person Dad wanted him to be. He was sweet and sensitive, kind and compassionate. He had re-treated into himself, into a world of fantasy and escape because it was too hard trying to be someone he wasn't, someone like Dad. Damon was unfairly born into conflict and heartache. While we all loved Damon, no one really paid him the attention he truly needed. And this was the result. All of Damon's silent strife had boiled over into violence and he hated himself for giving into it. But we were going to love him. I was going to fix it.

Mom put her hand up to the glass to calm Damon the best she could.

"Everything is going to be fine," she said. "Everything is going to be just fine."

I put my hand up next to Mom's hand and Damon met us with his from the other side.

"I'm going to get you out of here soon, okay?" I assured him as tears welled up in my eyes.

With that, Damon wiped his face clean and looked back at us with his typical gaze.

"They're all being really nice to me, Mom," he said. "Don't worry," he said, "I'm making friends."

We left that day, depleted, yet empowered to make things right.

In the following days, while waiting for Damon's hearing, I scrambled to organize a plan for when he was released. Right away, my sisters stepped back when I expected them to step up. I knew they were busy raising their kids, and to be quite honest, they weren't sure what to do. Neither was I, really, but in the time of Damon's need, I owed it to him to figure it out. I knew that this was my role. I was the quarterback and I always stayed in the game the longest. Even if one of them stepped up to try and help Damon, I probably wouldn't have let them. So, I didn't bother them, and decided that Damon would come live with me in Toledo upon his release. I prepared David, lined up a mentor for Damon and arranged visitation between them, and I prepared everything I could for the judge to convince him that my brother was a good person and that I'd take conscious care of him.

At the hearing, Damon was seated to the right of us at a desk facing the judge. Across from us was the attorney for the state. Damon kept his head hung, crying. The situation was overwhelming for him. Not knowing what the outcome would be kept tears of anxiety streaming. His remorse kept his head down.

We pled with the judge to dismiss Damon's charges. I recounted to him that Damon had never been a threat to anyone before this incident, and that I would be sure to help him resolve whatever thing had caused it. The sheriff stepped in as a witness on Damon's behalf and commented that Damon had exhibited excellent behavior while in custody and that so many people had showed up to visit him. So many people held a deep affinity for this boy and couldn't seem to conceive of what he'd done.

Before the judge could respond, I stood up. I had to make one more concession on Damon's behalf before any decisions were made.

"If I may, sir," I started, "I'm a law student at the University of Toledo, so I have some of the knowledge and access to resources needed to help rehabilitate my brother. I'll do whatever it takes, sir, to help him. I've already found him a mentor and scheduled him for counseling. I'll make sure he meets whatever expectations you see fit—community service, fines, retribution, whatever," I paused to look directly at the judge. "Just please, let me take my brother home with me today."

I sat back down and looked to Mom. The judge was thinking, his brow twisted up in contemplation. I was nervous for his decision because I knew that his considerations were different here in Fostoria than had we been anywhere else. Even if we were in Toledo or Youngstown, we wouldn't be going through this. The judge would've simply reprimanded Damon with first offense fines and some sort of probation. But this was Fostoria, and here, a seemingly disturbed young black boy posed a greater threat than just the severity of his crime.

"Mrs. Pinskey," the judge looked to Mom, "the allegations against your son indicate that he almost killed you. How can you feel safe if he is to go free?"

Mom stood, holding her chin up with reassurance, "I don't fear my son, your honor. I know he loves me and that this was a mistake. He's not a threat to nobody. My son's a good person, sir."

It wasn't quite the answer the judge was looking for.

"You know," he began, "it's not that I'm worried about Damon being a threat to you, Mrs. Pinskey. I have to consider whether or not Damon is a threat to others, to the community."

I filled up with apprehension. He couldn't keep Damon, he just couldn't.

The judge looked down at me, "I think we can work out a plan that makes sense. You're going to have to show me a realized plan of action. I want to see how many times he visits a counselor. I want to see their notes, their assessments, everything. I want to see progress. Do you understand?"

"Yes, sir," I said.

"Then, and only then, will I release Damon from probation," the judge continued. "And lastly, Damon may not return here. Keep him out of Fostoria and away from your mother until he has completed his rehabilitation plan," the judge finished, and turned his face away from us.

Sudden relief brought a smile to my face. We did it. Damon was free and coming to Toledo with me. As quickly as relief came, it disappeared again, and I felt fear set in. This was an enormous responsibility that five days ago I would've never dreamed of. *God, show me the way.*

When I picked up Damon, he shuffled to the car, ashamed. I hugged him tightly and ushered him into the passenger seat.

"Hey, you hungry?" I offered.

"Look, Diana," Damon started, "I'm so sorry you have to do this. I was stupid."

With such strong chagrin, Damon looked defeated. He assumed I was taking him because I had to, but he didn't understand that this was my plan all along. I could see that he couldn't shake his guilt yet. It would take time.

"Damon, it's okay," I looked over at him and waited for him to meet my eyes. "It's okay. We're going to make this work, alright? I love you very much."

Damon just nodded.

Deep down inside, beneath the veneer, I had no real plan. I didn't know what I was doing. I didn't know how this was going to work out with David, and I wasn't convinced that I was capable of totally taking care of Damon. But it was too late now, and regardless of my doubts, I never thought about turning back. Not for one minute. We took off quietly for Toledo—Damon sad, and I, scared.

Taking care of Damon was more work than I'd expected it to be. He wasn't self-sufficient yet. He hadn't been taught how to take care of himself properly, and it showed. Plus, it was difficult for David to adjust to having Damon in his house and I could see that. While David was gracious and granted me this favor, I felt bad for having to let my dysfunctional life intrude on our relationship.

David was hesitant but welcoming to Damon. He didn't know what the right things to do or say were, but his love for me kept him from giving up. David knew that I was desperate to help my brother, so he stood right behind me and supported me through it. Despite his love for me, David is just that type of person. His heart is huge and his love is pure.

David met us at the front door with a big smile and a loving hug that melted my anxieties.

"How's it going, Damon?" David shook his hand. I watched them scan each other and exchange greeting looks.

"Thank you for offering me your home. I'm glad to be here," Damon looked at David, shyly.

"No problem at all, man," David helped usher Damon into the house, his hand stretched out welcomingly. David took Damon's coat for him and assured him, "My home is your home, Damon."

David continued to flutter around, getting Damon situated, and making sure he had everything he would need. David treated Damon exactly how I expected him to—with love and kindness. Even if he had screaming doubts under the surface, he never let Damon know. But regardless of David's hospitable manners, Damon couldn't stop feeling like an imposition. He kept apologizing for his presence and mentioning that he didn't mean to intrude. It made it hard with Damon. He stayed so superficial, so closed off, so guilty looking. So, for the next eight days, that's how the three of us communicated at home—cordially and awkwardly, distant yet very polite.

I returned to school and rearranged my schedule to accommodate for Damon's upcoming appointments. He started with the psychologist a week after he'd moved in. At the time, I felt it imperative to be intimately involved in Damon's sessions. I was responsible for him. I was going to have to report back to the judge so I felt like I needed to be there, to know everything. More than that, I felt an obligation to be a part of the process and to try and hold Damon's hand through it. I wanted to be supportive, but that support was too overbearing and it was clear that Damon was uncomfortable with how I was treating him. Subtly, but obviously, Damon didn't like me stepping into his relationship with the therapist. Much like he hated that Mom had stepped in to take care of him after Dad died, Damon hated that I was doing the same thing—that I was bearing over him, making all of his decisions, trying to figure out his life for him. I should have listened to his cues to back away, but I didn't. I wanted to be helpful, despite Damon's desire to be left alone.

Over time, Damon did start to impose upon us because he was an irresponsible roommate and David grew frustrated with it. Damon would make a mess using the toilet, not clean up after himself, and he was careless with his things. The most obvious problem was Damon's hygiene. He didn't seem interested in being clean. When he woke up, he'd go into the bathroom and run the shower, but not actually wash. Then, without reservation, he'd quietly come downstairs, and plop down in front of the TV for the day. Every day. Day-in and day-out. I thought in the beginning that eventually, once he recovered from all that happened, Damon would start looking for a job, or at least ask me where to start. But he didn't. He did nothing. Our impression became that Damon had spent a lifetime learning this entitlement from my dad while also struggling with deep, complicated feelings that made him feel unworthy of being clean. The whole situation became more than I expected.

I sat Damon down and tried to address his hygiene habits with him.

"Damon, I know growing up we didn't have much time in the bathroom with everyone getting ready and all. But I'm thinking that there could be some things that you may consider after using the bathroom."

Damon looked at me, puzzled.

"We've noticed an odor, that we're not sure if you're aware of, that could go away if you make sure that you wash your hands and take a shower at night. What do you think?"

"Oh, do you think I smell?" Damon asked.

"Hey, man, I know how it is when you're rushing and moving fast," David interjected. I could tell that David wanted to relate to him, man to man. "Besides, us guys don't have much to worry about. But, you could do really well to just let me know if you need some soap or deodorant and we can get that for you. Whatever you need, we just want to help."

With that, I told Damon that he really needed to start looking for a job. I wasn't stern with him, but it felt strange to have this conversation with Damon because, after all, he was a grown man. I was foolish to think that it would be as easy as telling Damon to *shape up*. His problems, the problems that were now taking over our household, were products of deep seeded damage. Not only did Damon function differently, his mind had been ravaged over the years by my father and when Dad died, Damon was left to try and piecemeal some sort of understanding together. I imagine that everything was a conflict for him, and it showed in his actions. He loved Mom, yearned for her even, but still tried to hurt her. He was grateful to have me help him, but was building a resentment toward me for doing so. He felt entitled to live whichever way was comfortable for him, but he wasn't happy enough to take care of himself. Damon was a contradiction born from abuse, and I wasn't equipped to help him like I thought I was.

Nonetheless, I was determined, and I drew up a checklist of the things Damon needed to complete to move forward in life and to impress the judge.

For the next two months, he fought me. Tensions grew deeper as I reiterated over and over how he needed to conduct better hygiene and to be more responsible around the house. Mostly, he ignored me. But I persevered, and my first focus was getting Damon through his mandated counseling. I took him to his sessions every other day, and I started to sit outside of the office rather than try to barge in and be a part of things. Although I think Damon appreciated the space, he hated going altogether. He'd come out of the office when his session was over and give me a crooked smile before walking off to the car. In time, Damon completed the mandated number of sessions and we submitted everything to the court. Check.

Now it was on to getting Damon a job. Taking care of him, directing him through life, had become a second job for me. I was already working at a law firm as a legal assistant while going to law school at night. I was quite busy. I figured I'd built a strong enough reputation with some folks at the firm to see if Damon could get some type of work there too. We perfected his resume together and submitted his application. The firm hired Damon to be a runner which meant that he worked on filings and completed deliveries. Mary Beth Morgan, the office administrator, was so kind to give my brother a job. She, and the entire firm, accepted Damon without hesitation. They made Damon feel like he was part of a team, and they never judged him or our circumstance. Chris and Steve Snyder were a godsend. They always joked around with Damon. They shared stories with him. They ate lunch with him and allowed him to be a part of their "inner circle" outside of work as well. I couldn't have asked for anything more. Things were looking up. Check.

The list continued. Once Damon had a job, was released from probation, and obtained a driver's license, I thought it might be time for him to find some independence—to move out and live on his own, like an adult. Of course, I would continue to support him and be there for whatever he needed, but I had done as much as I could for him, and Damon clearly wasn't happy living with me and David anyway. A classmate of mine was trying to sublet her apartment before summer vacation so I proposed that she rent to Damon. She agreed and Damon moved into his own apartment at the end of the semester. He was so excited.

I didn't expect Damon to cling to his independence so quickly or so fiercely. He instantly grew as distant from me as he'd been when we were kids. I never heard from him. He didn't ask for anything. Only sometimes, I'd see him walking.

I would drive up to him and roll down the window, "Hey, need a ride?"

"No, I want to walk," he'd say, keeping his gaze focused forward.

It seemed like he severed ties with me after all I had done for him. I would see Damon laughing with the guys at work so I'd go over to join them and he'd stop talking, instantly. I tried to chalk it up to him being embarrassed of his big sister and wanting to feel separate from me, but that was a juvenile rationale that kept me from noticing what perhaps the real problems might have been. Damon wanted to live his own life, devoid of us.

I backed off. I let Damon live how he wanted to, and I could see some light in the darkness for him then. In the coming weeks, Damon lost about thirty pounds and he looked amazing. He started to eat right and began to exercise more. One time, I saw him running near the University of Toledo when I was headed to class. He didn't notice me drive by. I just smiled. When I saw him at work, his smile seemed brighter. He walked with more confidence than I had ever seen him walk with before. He faced people with better posture, and one day, he even let me pick him up for work. Damon cut off all of his hair and it accented his face beautifully.

"Well, you're looking mighty fine," I joked with him.

Damon looked at me out of the corner of his eye and gave a half-smile. I felt relieved in the hope that Damon was getting better. That with his independence, he found himself, and I wasn't going to take that away from him. I could feel a new excitement coming from him and that made me think that maybe I hadn't screwed up so badly after all. Damon was going to be okay. We were all going to be okay.

CHAPTER TEN

seventy times seven

As Damon seemed to get better, I realized that I had dug my own life in to a rut. While trying to lift him up, I let myself down. I was tired from working so much, I was tired in the aftermath of my brother's struggle, and my grades had plummeted almost to the point of no return. The moment that I stopped and realized all the destruction that lay in the path behind me, the world started to spin again. I had come so far. I had come so far from that little broken house in Fostoria, from that little broken girl, to law school, to success and security. But now it seemed to be slipping away. I couldn't juggle it all and I was disappointed in myself. Maybe I was a fraud. *Maybe I'm not good enough for this.* I felt like a fake because I wasn't good enough to catch up. I was so far behind, so crushed under the weight of my own expectations—not just for myself, but for Damon too—that I felt like I lost it all.

As I sloughed into work, distraught and reeling, I was sat down by a couple of the firm's attorneys and told that I couldn't write. They said that I wasn't getting any better like they'd expected me to. It broke my heart. I was already kicking myself inside for having let my grades fall and for letting my life turn to rubble so that Damon could have what he needed. Then I come to work to hear two attorneys who I admire, who I am working to become like, tell me that I'm not good enough. I didn't know what to say. I knew they liked me as a person, and I just sat there, hoping they would still give me a chance. You know, like a charity case.

I sank deep down. I wanted to be really great at something. I wanted to be bigger than life, to turn the extreme grief I came to know so intimately as a child into unbounding positivity and success. I thought I could do it all, and year after year, it kept turning out that I couldn't. *Maybe law school just isn't for me. Maybe this is the wrong dream. Why am I here anyway?*

I had to look outside of myself to make it better. *What else am I good at?* I thought back to when I modeled for some quick cash. I was good at it, and I only stopped because I thought that law school was "better and more important." Swiftly, I contacted my agent. She knew exactly how to lift my spirits. She assured me that if I were to dedicate to it, that I could have a future in the modeling industry. She told me I could make it in New York City. She told me that she believed in me. She said that she had a vision for my future that didn't just involve modeling, but acting too.

"You should really tryout for commercials," she said, "and television."

That lifted me out of the rut in my head and catapulted me into daydreams of beautiful stardom. I jumped at her words. *That's what I'll do*, I thought. *I'll fly to New York. I'll go on go-see's. I'll get signed by a big, big agency and drop out of law school. That's it.* Flawless plan. There was no doubt in my impulsive mind that this would succeed. I could make it big this way. Bulletproof plan.

I was ecstatic to get started, to do this for myself, but first, I had to tell Damon. I was technically still in charge of his wellbeing, and even if he was avoiding me these days, I was the only person he could rely on. I wouldn't just abandon him. In fact, maybe New York could be the break my brother needed. I didn't want him to feel trapped in Toledo without me, and he couldn't go back to Fostoria, so why not come with me to New York? When I figured this was how things would go, the plan only seemed sweeter to me. Me and my brother in the big city. Survivors. Making our success.

I took the rest of the summer to make my arrangements and think through each facet of my plan. As August began, the next semester neared and fall approached, so I met Damon at work to tell him my plan. I grabbed him with excitement and told him all about my idea. I told him that I wanted him to come with me and that we'd be so happy in New York. I promised to help him, support him, and that I was going to make it big as a model. I couldn't wait for us to get started and the time was now.

Damon looked at me blankly for a moment. "No, I'm good," was all he said.

What? I couldn't believe it. All of my positivity and adrenaline was sucked out of my body, leaving my jaw hanging open. He dismissed me so quickly.

"You're good?" I retorted. "What do you mean, 'No?'"

I huffed at him a little bit. I could feel myself getting upset so I took a deep breath, waiting for his response. I didn't want to snap at him. I just had a hard time helping it.

"I mean, I'm good here. I've just gotten through everything, just gotten through probation. New York's not for me. I have other places I want to go."

Damon spoke casually, like he had a plan he hadn't told me about. And that kind of offended me more. I just kept trying to bring him closer to me, and all the while, he cast himself farther and farther away. I felt like I was offering him a giant opportunity here and he was refusing to take it. But Damon didn't want what I wanted for him, and I couldn't come to terms with that. At the time, I didn't value what he wanted. I didn't believe that he really knew. My emotions boiled over. I couldn't stop them. A part of me wanted to step away, forget about him, and just go. But a bigger part of me worried about leaving him by himself. I couldn't do that. *What if something happens?* But at this point, I also couldn't stay.

"Well, then," I tapped my foot and fidgeted with frustration, "what will you do? Who will you stay with? How are you going to pay rent?" I asked him questions rapid fire, trying to prove that he had to come with me. I persisted, but I wasn't persuading him, probably only pushing him farther away.

"I'll figure it out," Damon said.

I couldn't let up. All of my plans depended on Damon coming with me. I brought him this far, and now, I couldn't let him tear this away from me. What else would I do? Stay and fail?

"What do you mean you'll figure it out, Damon? I've done all your figuring out for you. You can't do it on your own," I snapped. I said things I shouldn't have, but the words were spilling out of my mouth like molasses. Slow and ugly.

"Look," Damon lashed back, "thank you for helping me, okay? But I'm tired of being babied. I don't need your help anymore, Diana. I can take care of myself."

He wouldn't relent. He wouldn't change his mind, and here came another dose of molasses, filling my mouth before pouring out.

"Well, you did a terrible job of keeping up your apartment. I know. She told me it needs cleaned out!" I stuck my nose up at him, trying to prove that he needed me, but with words like that, who would want me? I kept it up, "You have a lot to work on, Damon. A lot." I was trying to force him to see that he needed to be how I thought he should be, but I'd lost all cogency now.

This wasn't the way to get through to Damon at all.

He tried to back me off, tried to escape the conversation.

"I'm sick and tired of you telling me what to do! I'm sick of this shit, Diana. I'm sick of you looking down on me, treating me like I can't do anything. Sick of it. Please."

But I had to drive the stake in for a final blow.

"Well, I'm sick of you."

More was coming. Something worse. I didn't even know it was coming until it was there, until the words were floating in the air around us, reverberating, beating on both of us.

"Let's be real, Damon. You know what you did to Mom. That's why we're here anyway, isn't it?"

My lips puckered up with disgust, and I stopped talking. I just stared at him, waiting for retaliation, out of breath and out of mind.

I hurt Damon. His shoulders drooped down and he looked away from me. He reassumed his old body language, his defeated slump. I was too busy thinking about myself to fully realize the damage I'd done. I was too selfish.

"Now, look," I told Damon with a hushed sternness, "when I get back, I expect that you will have the apartment cleaned so that we can move you out. Then, we'll pack for New York. So, just be ready when I get back, okay?" I wasn't going to take any of his excuses.

Damon didn't even react. He just slightly nodded his head, but wouldn't look at me. He had shut off.

I stormed off.

I packed my things furiously. I shoved a jumbled assortment of clothes into my suitcase while I mulled over our argument in my mind. I was so angry that Damon thought he could just take care of himself. As irrational of a thing that is to be mad about, I couldn't help it. I'd spent so much time, worked so hard to help him, and now, all of a sudden, he didn't need me? I should've congratulated myself for having given him the tools to grow into this new, independent version of himself, but I didn't. I was so tied to being Damon's caretaker that I couldn't let him go when I needed to the most.

I was so selfish, but I couldn't see it.

The phone rang. It was Mom.

The first thing she asked me was, "Have you spoken to Damon lately?"

Every word in that question irritated me. With little honesty and a lot of sarcasm, I told her that he was fine.

"Just let him be, Mom. That's what he wants right now. *To be on his own.*" I said the last part mockingly.

Although mom didn't know about our argument, the inflection in my voice probably gave it away. She could hear my frustration. Coupled with that was an unsettling feeling. She said she couldn't get Damon off her mind and needed me to check in on him.

"I hear you, Diana, but why don't you just go by his place before you leave. Just go check on him really quick."

Reluctantly, I agreed.

"And call me and let me know," Mom added.

It infuriated me. To me, Damon just went out of his way to tell me how much he didn't want me checking on him anymore, how much he didn't need my help, and how he could take care of himself. As soon as I decided to accept that and quietly leave without him, Mom made me go back to do the exact thing he hated me for. But it wasn't worth fighting about, and I wouldn't lie to her. I'd just stop by in the morning, make sure Damon had what he needed, and then go catch my flight.

August 12th, 1994.

I knocked on Damon's door several times.

"Damon," I screamed, "I know you're in there."

There was no answer.

"Call Mom. She wants to talk to you, okay?"

I could hear his morning alarm going off.

"Damon?"

I wasn't surprised that he wouldn't answer me, and I wasn't about to waste any more time on this battle. He was hurt and angry, and so was I. If he wanted to ignore me for a little while, maybe that was better for the both of us. I wanted to grant Damon the time to cool down, give him his space like he'd asked for. I sighed and waited another moment before leaving. *I'll call him later.*

I met Erica to head out to the airport. She agreed to come with me to NYC. On our way, I thought about how I might apologize to Damon when I called him later.

Erica and I checked our luggage and sat waiting for our flight. I faded into the thought of getting to NYC. This was it. My new chance. I was bubbling with excitement. I couldn't wait to get into New York City, to see all of it, to explore everything. I sat there, daydreaming about walking down the runway. *Diana Jackson*, superstar. It was all going to happen this time. Law school might have gone bust, but this plan wouldn't.

As our plane started to board, I heard my name being called over the terminal loudspeaker.

Paging, Diana Pinskey. Paging, Diana Pinskey. There's a call for you. Please, pick up a white courtesy phone. Diana Pinskey, please pick up a white courtesy phone.

I alerted the clerk taking boarding passes that I'd been called to take a phone call before lightly jogging to the courtesy phone up the hall. When I answered, I heard my aunt on the line.

"Diana," her voice was rushed and labored, "Diana, it's Damon."

"What?" I cupped my other ear to hear her better. I pushed against the receiever, "What about Damon?"

Then the strangest and worst words were said to me.

"He jumped, Diana. He jumped off an overpass bridge."

Stop.

Everything stopped. I couldn't grasp what my aunt just said to me. My whole body started to thump. Everything started to drown into static. *Don't say what I think you're saying.*

"Are you sure?" I came back. "Did you ask if someone pushed him? What did he say? Is he okay? Where is he now?"

"Diana," my aunt stopped me.

"Well, is he okay?" I demanded, tears starting to stream down my face. I just wanted her to answer my questions. "Did he get hurt?" I kept up.

"Diana, stop," my aunt took a stern tone with me.

And then there was a pause.

"Sweetie," she started.

"No," I groaned as pain mounted in my chest.

"He didn't make it. Damon's dead."

The world evaporated from around me right then. My entire body buckled from beneath me and I dropped the phone, screaming. I thrashed on the airport floor, yelling out for Damon, yelling out to God, unable to understand what was happening. I was choking on tears and hyperventilation, crumbling from

a hysteria that was building. "We were the only African-Americans in this school and you knew what went on. How could you not have known? And you didn't stop them! No one stopped them from hurting Damon!" I took a breath. I was crying again. "Everyone hurt Damon! Everyone! And now he's gone," I broke into a sob.

Mr. Holman let me say all of the things that I needed to. I told him that I blamed him and all of the teachers for turning a blind eye to our torment. I told him that he should have protected Damon; that that was his responsibility. I told him that he could've stopped the bullying and that he didn't do what he could've done for Damon. He didn't do what he was supposed to.

He didn't argue with what I said or try to justify anything, but he did apologize. Mr. Holman sat with me and consoled me. We talked for some time about Damon's suicide and about what pushed him to it. For as much rage as I had toward him and St. Wendelin, Mr. Holman promised me that he'd help me to honor Damon, and that he'd work hard to not let this happen to other students. He promised me that he would make up for having ignored Damon's abuse by helping me start a memorial scholarship for students to stand up for one another as a means to stop bullying. I decided to call it a character scholarship. Together, we'd heal through charity, and maybe we could find some peace in our mistakes knowing that someone else's brother might be saved by this scholarship. God brought together two guilty people so that they might find redemption together.

When I got home, my sisters were all bickering. I stood in the doorway listening to them. They were all fighting about which kind of chicken they should order and when we'd be eating. Lola was trying to calm down Toni who was snapping at Janelle and Cheryl while Andrea was on the phone, shushing all of them as she tried to change her flight to get home earlier.

"What are you doing?" I stopped them. The gravity of it all came crashing down on me. We'd all been brought together because of our little brother's death, yet we couldn't come together over it. After moving out of our parents' house, we separated not just physically but in spirit. The six of us had changed, grown into different people, but in the wake of the biggest tragedy of our lives, I expected us all, as sisters, to unite, even if it was in sorrow. I just shook my head at them all, moved by their ability to gloss over Damon's suicide, to selfishly argue about chicken right now. I didn't tell them about Mr. Holman.

In that moment, we heard a knock on the door. Mom opened the door and a uniformed officer handed her a box. To our surprise, it was my brother's belongings.

Silence hit us. We all went to the front room.

Mom sat in the middle of the room with us surrounding her. She opened the box and the first thing she pulled out was a pair of jeans that looked like they were cut completely down the middle. They were Damon's jeans. They were blood stained. We all cried. We were all humbled in that moment. The thought of what actually happened to Damon hit us again. We held hands, crying, as Mom pulled out each piece of clothing. We were devastated.

I never moved to New York. After a few days, I went back to Toledo and did the best I could to catch up. I never thought it was actually going to work out. I fully expected to fail law school seeing as how dim the future looked now. *How am I going to get through?* I was so distracted by Damon's gruesome death, haunted inexorably by my past, and depressed like I'd never been before. I couldn't rise above it all, and for the first time, I didn't have any hope left that I would. That big voice that comes from deep inside wouldn't go away and I stopped arguing with it. *Who are you trying to fool? It's over for you. You can't do this. Look how stupid you are. You don't deserve to live.*

I moved back home to help my mom. Yes. I moved back to the house I grew up in. It was challenging to move back to that house, but I had to do it. I had to help my mom. I had to block out everything that I felt from my past, even though just walking upstairs was suffocating at times. I just kept focused on Mom. Besides, I wanted to be with her to let her know that she could count on me, that I would be there for her, but wouldn't you know it, she was there for me.

Mom started writing me notes again just like when I was in high school, except this time, the notes weren't in my track shoes. They were wherever Mom knew I'd be—on my bathroom mirror, on the door leading to my car, on the window above the sink where I washed dishes. She tried to give me all the strength that she could.

June 21, 1995

Just a note to tell you to keep the faith, hang on in there, and finally, be strong. Wait on the Lord for continued guidance about your studying. The Lord, Jesus Christ, will see your pathway where you can run and not be weary, walk and not faint. Remember when you are weak, He (Jesus) will be strong. He will make a way out of no way when it comes to your studies. He will give you the ability to have retention untold.

There were times I'd go to the library to "study," but what I really did was sink deeper then. I just needed a quiet space to do it. I would find a study room and take in a bunch of books that I had no intention of reading, and I'd stare. I would just sit there and stare at nothing and let self-deprecation wash over my mind. The only person I talked to anymore was God, and in the study room, I would pray. My prayer was always the same.

WHY? Why, God, why?

When the answer didn't come, I simply asked for strength.

School was so difficult. Life was so difficult. Thankfully, I had Mom encouraging me and cheering me on. Only she knew about the pain we shared, but she didn't know about my argument with Damon. No one knew about the deep darkness that swallowed me whole most days. It was just me and God. Because, honestly, I didn't want anyone to know anything. I talked to my sisters from time to time and Lola always allowed me to cry on her shoulder, but I didn't go too deep. I was still ashamed. The only way to survive was to push through it alone, not spread it around. The depth and intricacy of my darkness became strange at times, and my grades were proof that my stamina had been ripped out of me. It all became too embarrassing to ever talk about.

When my mind didn't start to heal with time, I feared I was going crazy. I was convinced there was something mentally wrong me, that something was broken inside of me. There was a debilitating weight bearing down in my brain and I knew that if I didn't fix it, it might become irreversible. Even in the brief moments when I felt some relief, I still couldn't focus my attention or rally my motivation enough to improve my grades, so I went to see a psychologist. I needed help.

The psychologist was a petite, middle-aged woman with an inviting demeanor and an office with so much wood that it reeked of Pine Sol. I didn't know what we were going to do or how this was going to work out, but I told her about the darkness. Reluctantly, I told her everything about how I felt and that I couldn't understand why this was happening to me. She had to of seen the desperation in my face.

After a moment of consideration, she started asking me a laundry list of questions.

"Have you had any serious trauma in your life lately? Any deaths in the family? Anyone diagnosed with serious illness? Any big moves or problems at home?"

Yes.

"Is there any trauma in your past? Abuse? Illness?"

Yes.

It dawned on me where this was going.

"Well," I started, "yes, my brother, Damon." I went on to tell her about how my brother attacked Mom, how he came to live with me, and lastly, how he killed himself.

The doctor stared at me for a moment, awe struck.

"Wow," she was taken aback. "That is serious. Did you take some time off from school?"

"No," I answered.

"How have you been coping with the grieving process?" her head was cocked to one side and she leaned forward toward me.

"Well, I cried a lot," I looked down at my hands.

"But have you *grieved?*" she asked me with emphasis, but I didn't know what she meant.

I looked at her curiously.

The doctor explained to me that dealing with trauma can inflict an array of long-term effects on a person, and that a grieving process would help me to cope with what I had been through. There would be no set time assigned to this process—I just needed to deal with all of the grief in my life.

It may seem naïve that this was a new concept to me, but I had never thought of things in this way. When I thought about how much trauma and grief had truly stricken my life, I was scared to even think about hashing all of that out. Sure, tough and scary things happened, and Damon's death turned my world inside out, but what choice is there other than to just keep going? *If I'm choosing to live, then I'm choosing to move on, right?* I just wanted to drift on and not have to explain anything. I just wanted to keep moving forward. It was the only way that I knew.

The therapist went on to talk about words like *suppression* and *anxiety* and wanted to explore how the trauma in my life might be holding me back or making me depressed. For me, though, from what I understood her definition of suppression to mean, suppression was survival.

After a while and after conceding that I couldn't live inside of my head anymore, I agreed to delve in. In the back of my mind, I wanted to believe that I just had some kind of disease, a mental disorder that maybe she could simply give me a pill for. I wished that were the case because the internal work to be done was hard. I had to sift through pain buried deep inside of me, dig it up, dissect it, and then repair it—but I became committed to that process.

I sought out self-help books and became immersed in Tony Robbins and Zig Ziglar. I learned different techniques to help push me through and to stay on track to wellness. I attended conferences, read books, wrote daily, and ran constantly. My runs became more intense and more frequent and I learned how to connect more deeply with my thoughts through deep breathing. I was persevering and for the first time in a long time, I could feel it. I could feel my vitality come back. I was learning truths about myself, about Dad, about Damon, and about life that were invaluable and necessary for my mental health. I re-engaged in school and juggled everything the best way I could. I was getting better, I was finding some peace, and I was enjoying the journey. I could finally say that I couldn't believe God brought me this far.

During my healing, the big thing that remained difficult for me to correctly navigate was my love life. I loved David and he was there for me through everything with my brother. David let me put him on the backburner so that I could find my way through the devastation. He supported me when I needed it and he did all the things that any loving partner should. The problem was never with him. It was always with me. The connection between us was so natural since the beginning. I could always rely on David. He was my strength. But David was always the lover and I the beloved. I kept it that way on purpose. It was difficult for me to pay him the attention that he deserved and to let him in as wholly as he wanted me to. Even though we lived together, I kept myself at a distance from him, just in case. I struggled to make time for David and he, rightfully so, struggled to understand why. But I'd insulated myself from others for so long that it was hard for me to let him into my space. In a way, it frustrated me that David made me care so much about him because I was terrified of what that could mean one day. I knew I wanted to marry this man, but especially after Damon's death, I couldn't find it in me to let David in. We went on like this throughout the rest of my time in law school.

Once I graduated, my attention turned solely to passing the bar exam. I channeled everything I had into studying for that exam. I would recite affirmations to myself and I had to carry the belief that I *would* pass. There was no choice to fail. I studied non-stop. There wasn't any time for anything else— not my mental health, not my family, not David. My boss offered me full-time work if I passed the exam the first time so the pressure to do so was huge.

I sat for the bar in Columbus and I left out of there feeling a confused mixture of hope and anxiety. I'd worked so hard. There was no way I failed.

But I did. I failed. I was devastated, and all of the voices that I thought I had worked out of my head came back to insult me. After hearing my results, everything around me started to spiral again. I didn't earn the full-time position I was so excited for, and to think that I would have to go through the process of retaking the bar was overwhelming. Again, I wondered, *Have I made all the wrong decisions? What am I doing?*

Nights became challenging again. I harbored a deep yearning that burned from inside of me. I felt like I'd never reach anything. My entire life up to this point seemed to always teeter on the cusp, and in the sprint to the finish line, I'd always fall behind. I never seemed to win the race. I began to shut everything and everyone out again, and I succumbed to the depression that I had bonded with so well in the past. I couldn't peel myself out of the slump I'd fallen into. I couldn't even fathom taking the bar again. *How am I going to do this?*

Mom asked me if I had been praying and reading my Bible. I told her I had, but the truth was that I hadn't been as focused as usual. I'd been neglecting my faith, just like everything else. Then I thought about early mornings back home and sitting quietly on the top step, listening to Mom turn the pages of her Bible while whispering to God. I'd forgotten what those moments felt like and how much I admired Mom in those times. Her heart was so heavy with turmoil yet she made sure to take the time to commune with God every morning, alone. She survived because of it.

Out of sheer desperation and repentance, I went back to church and committed to praying more often. I searched through my Bible for answers and quickly, the scriptures began to fill the void inside of me. God spoke to me through His Word. I just had to pursue it.

I thought about Mom's notes in my shoes. I thought about them in a whole new way. I'd collected all of the notes she wrote me when I moved back home after Damon died, and I started to cling to them as though they were life to me now.

The more I read my Bible and clung to Mom's notes, the brighter a light shone inside of me and illuminated all of the dark spaces that were dragging me down. I found atonement in the scriptures and it invigorated me to keep going, to keep trying, to follow through, and to take the bar exam again. This time, things would be different.

I decided that before I could study for the bar exam again, I needed to reassess what was going on in my life. Not just at the surface level, but deep down, like I had before. I needed to keep my mind and my soul in check and right with God before slipping back into that dark, desperate place of self-loathing that I had come to know so well. I needed to move out of David's house. At the time, I never felt like we were doing the right thing, but I liked living with David so I convinced myself with excuses that it was okay—*I need to save money. I can't afford to live in the dorms. I failed the bar and don't have a job.* But now, I needed to be straight up with myself and that meant living the way that I believed was right for me. I prayed a lot because I knew I actually couldn't afford to live on my own.

Shortly thereafter, I was shocked to get a paycheck in the mail from a modeling job I'd done months before and forgot about. It was enough for the deposit and first month's rent for my own apartment. That was enough of a sign from God for me.

David was so confused. I was leaving him again, and I can imagine that my decision made him feel less important than he truly was to me. In fact, moving into my own apartment was actually a turning point for me, but he couldn't see it that way. I chose commitment. I was making a pledge to the right things—to not giving up on myself and passing the bar, to success, and to David. I wasn't leaving to be with anybody else. I was leaving because I needed to be with myself before I could properly commit to him.

As I expected, David stayed committed to me. No matter what, he always saw things through for me. When I got into my apartment, I only wanted the bare essentials. David gave me a table and chair, I bought some forks, plates, and two cups from Target, a couple of hangers, two towels, a mattress, and a cardboard dresser. That was it. I taped up positive affirmation posters and scriptures all over the walls.

Even when I walk through the darkest valley, I will not be afraid, for you are close beside me. Your rod and your staff protect and comfort me. Psalm 23:4

Be strong and courageous. Do not be afraid; do not be discouraged, for the LORD your God will be with you wherever you go. Joshua 1:9

Every accomplishment starts with the decision to try.

Keep Jesus first, you will always be first.
Keep Jesus second, you will always be last.

You passed the bar exam – CLAIM IT!

Believe it – God has plans for you that always work out for good – no matter what it looks like right now.

No weapon formed against me shall prosper.

Trust in the LORD with all your heart; do not depend on your own understanding. Seek His will in all you do, and He will show you which path to take. Proverbs 3:5-6

I crossed out the score on my bar exam results, wrote in a new score and hung that up too. I hung it right in front of the table I studied at. Honestly, my apartment looked crazy. It was another planet inside that place. Scriptures and affirmations were everywhere. I lived, breathed, and ate the bar exam. When I had to do other things like cook food or shower, I'd read the posters all over the walls out loud to motivate myself. I might have crossed that fine line where determination turns into obsession. Nothing mattered besides passing the bar.

I established a routine. Every morning, I would pray, read my Bible, journal my thoughts, walk down to Maxwell's Brew for a café mocha, walk back to the house, cook breakfast, and then start studying by taking old bar exams. It was my ritual. I took a timed exam every single day, and if I got frustrated, I'd recite one of the scriptures or affirmations hanging on my wall. For every question I got wrong on an exam, I'd handwrite the right answer. After morning study time, I took a hard three mile run at Ottawa Park, and then ate lunch. After that, I spent the rest of the day studying, taking one more short break for dinner. All the while, throughout my day, I would pray, read the scriptures and affirmations plastered all over my walls, and listen to classical music. I never broke routine. It was just me and God for two whole months.

I learned a lot about commitment in that time. When you're committed, there's no congratulatory procession. There's no special attention, no one to coach you or to keep you motivated. Commitment doesn't come dressed up like that. Commitment just does. It keeps going despite all obstacles, despite adversity. It pushes through tears and disappointment, through pain and exhaustion. Commitment is work. Commitment doesn't have sympathy for you, and it doesn't make excuses. Commitment doesn't blame other people. Commitment doesn't allow you to crumble under pressure. It beckons every single layer of your being to dig deep, to trust God's Word, to have faith, and to find the strongest part of your character to push you to keep moving. Commitment pays the toll, no matter what.

Soon I would learn to make the biggest commitment of my life.

David and I often played pick up ball at the rec center so when he called and asked me to take a break from my studies to join him, I didn't think anything of it. When he came to pick me up, I told David that I only had about an hour to play. I told him that I really needed to focus on some portions of the bar exam that were particularly challenging.

"Okay, but first, I want you to try on these shoes."

David knew that the best way to my heart was to buy me a pair of basketball or running shoes. We hadn't seen each other a lot and I figured he wanted to give me these because he knew I was working hard. A smile grew across my face from cheek to cheek.

I looked at the box and immediately noticed they were the wrong size.

"Oh, I wear elevens," I looked up at David, still grateful.

"Well, just try them on," he motioned for me to take them out of the box. "Just to see."

"Why should I try them on? I'm certain these won't fit, but thank you anyway."

David became impatient. Sternly, he asserted, "I insist that you at least try them on. What harm is it? Just try them on."

"Okay," I said, wondering, *What's his deal?* "I'll try them on."

I sat back down, feeling a bit irritated because I knew I had to get back to studying. We weren't going to have barely any time for our game now. I opened the box.

"I love the color. Very nice!" I smiled at David.

"Try the left one on first."

Awkwardly, I agreed. I looked at him suspiciously. *Why is he insisting on which shoe I try on?* I hurried to try on the left shoe, quickly untying the strings, when I noticed something was stuck to the shoe and bobbing upward. I squinted to see what it was.

A ring. A beautiful diamond ring.

David knelt down in front of me.

"Diana Pinskey, will you marry me and be my wife?"

Immediately, my hand shot over my mouth. I gasped for air as tears instantly poured down my face. I was overwhelmed. In that moment, I felt all was well in the world. The love of my life just proposed to me. Nothing could be better.

As I look back on this, I'm amazed at how it all came together. I never told David about Mom's notes in my track shoes and the impact they had on my life, yet David proposed to me with a ring in my shoe.

Ironic? I think not. God has a way of making all things beautiful.

Diana and David, 1990.

Diana, modeling photo.

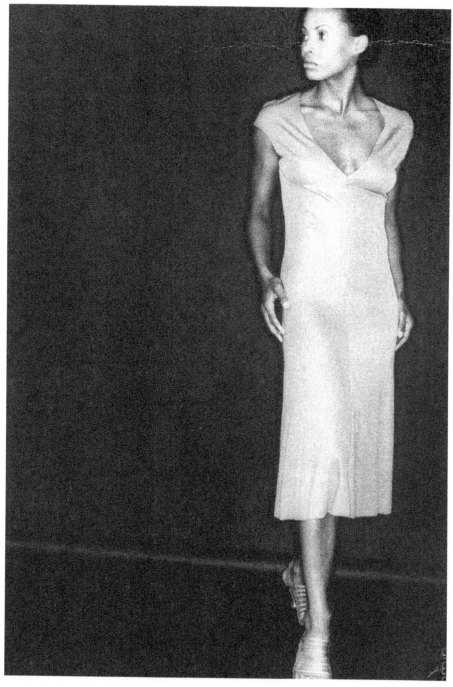

Diana, modeling photo.

Diana, modeling photo.

DAY Monday　　　DATE 1/17/94

After shoveling snow for an hour around the neighborhood, I finally have some money in pocket. I have earned a total $15.00 which I will soon spend after a little rest. I only wish there was a way to keep on getting more.

DAY Monday　　　DATE 1/24/94

I can not live this life anymore. Tommorrow, I shall be free of my overbearing mother and this pathetic joke of a world. After Tommorrow, when I go around town and out for one day, I shall return. Alas, hot and snow shovel, take one final look at the new comics + whatever else I need to take of before leaving this world at last. Tommorrow, will be my Day of Death. Who am I kidding? I won't kill myself now but one day I shall be free of this world.

This is the last page of Damon's journal.

6-21-95
1:19 pm

Dear Di.

Just a note to tell
you to keep the faith,
hang on in there and
finally, Be Strong Ep6:10
Wait on the Lord for continued
guidance about your studying
The Lord Jesus Christ will
see you through. He light
up your pathway where
you can run and not fall

Notes Mom started to leave for me again after Damon passed.

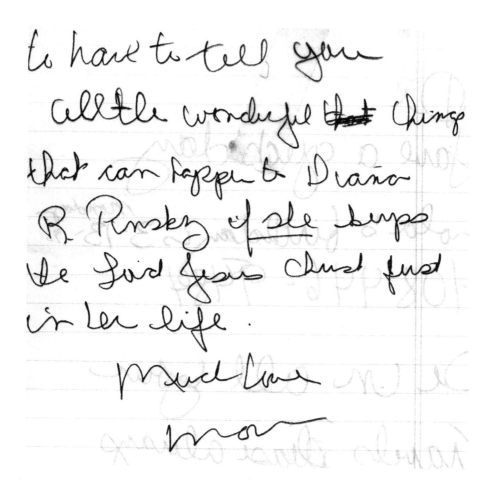

Mom always said, "Keep the Lord, Jesus Christ, first so that you can always be first. If you put Him second, you'll always be last."

son
10-13-93

hello di,

love ya much
just remember the Lord Jesus
Christ will provide.

Be still and know that I
am God" — psalm 46:10
listen for his voice

They who wait on the Lord
Shall renew their strength
Isaiah 40:31
time for a refueling in the Lord Jesus

God Love You.

I Love You,

just some thoughts
on Today, mom

Mom actually wrote this to me in 1994 while Damon was living with me and
David and I were in law school. I didn't know how I was going to make it.

David, 1990.

Diana and Damon, law school "Casino Night" fundraiser.

UT's Pinskey Runs Her Way From Track To Law School

By Keith Wade
Collegian Sports Writer

Diana Pinskey is the former Rocket record holder in the outdoor triple jump, and is currently the record holder in the indoor triple jump 38-1/4. She finished seventh at the MAC championship this past weekend, and was nominated for the Scholar-Athlete of the year award here at the University of Toledo.

After accomplishing all of this, Pinskey, a senior with one more year of eligibility left, is hanging up her spikes.

"I really would like to keep on running, because I feel I am just starting to peak," Pinskey said. "But I plan on going to law school in August and it would be almost impossible to balance running, working, an attending law school at the same time."

Pinskey, who is scheduled to graduate in August with a bachelor's degree in Legal Administrative Services, says she is very happy about the way her career went at UT.

"I feel I am much more confident in myself, and I have grown a lot as a person since I have been here," Pinskey said. "Overall, the team has grown immensely. We are a complete team now and we realize it takes a complete team effort to win."

Pinskey, who hails from Fostoria, Ohio, says her biggest accomplishment at UT has been being able to balance working as a legal assistant at Owens-Illinois Inc., running, and keeping her grade point above a 3.0 average.

"I didn't have a social life, all my time was allocated," Pinskey said. "Actually, I don't have to work, but it is good experience and I enjoy my job, so it wasn't that bad."

At Owens-Illinois, Pinskey already has her own computer, phone, and office, yet she is far from satisfied.

"I am happy with my office, but I know if I keep going in school, I can do a lot better," Pinskey said. "After law school, I want to work in Personal Injury-Malpractice or as a Corporate Lawyer, I would also like to get married sometime in the near future."

In the little free time Pinskey will have, she plans on staying in shape.

"I will do some running during the summer," Pinskey said. "I also would like to do some road races to stay in shape."

Pinskey says now that her com-

Diana Pinskey

petitive career is over, she will miss the running.

"I know I am going to miss the competition," Pinskey said. "But, I will not miss the workouts."

When Pinskey leaves UT, she would like to be remembered as an athlete who really matured over the years, and a good student that got along well with everyone.

The Collegian. May, 1990

Damon, high school graduation photo.

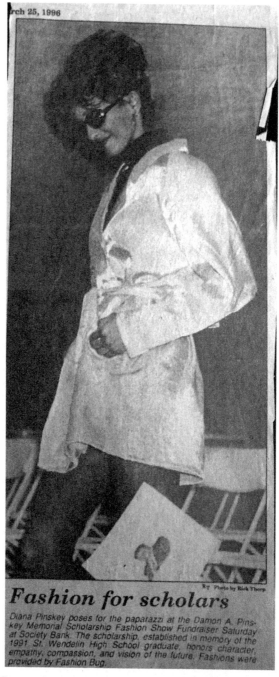

rch 25, 1996

Photo by Rick Thorp

Fashion for scholars

Diana Pinskey poses for the paparazzi at the Damon A. Pinskey Memorial Scholarship Fashion Show Fundraiser Saturday at Society Bank. The scholarship, established in memory of the 1991 St. Wendelin High School graduate, honors character, empathy, compassion, and vision of the future. Fashions were provided by Fashion Bug.

After Damon's passing, I established a character scholarship at St. Wendelin in his memory. This is Janelle modeling for a fundraiser we held, 1996.

PART THREE

CHAPTER TWELVE
convalescent

Look after each other so that none of you fails to receive the grace of God. Watch out that no poisonous root of bitterness grows up to trouble you, corrupting many.
Hebrews 12:15

You know already that my father was a terror. He was a cruel, indignant man who inflicted heinous pain on all of us. But like I've said, I came at the end of his wrath, once he'd grown tired and sick, after he'd already spent a decade preying upon my older sisters. I spent so much time in the dark about who my father really was although I felt the deep sting of his abuse all the same. Through the years, my love for my father wavered because there was a fluidity to my impression of him. He'd done unforgiveable things, but I also wanted him to love me. There were just so many things that I didn't understand as a child.

Part of the reason I had trouble understanding so much around me was because my sisters protected me. I know that now. They hadn't had anyone come before them, anyone to shield them from the horrors of my dad's twisted mind. They were so practiced. They knew, for the most part, how to navigate around Dad's wrath and how to carry me through as mildly scathed as possible. They kept things from me. They hid truths. They whispered away from me, processed their feelings with each other secretly. They shielded me, and I am forever grateful to them.

I didn't come to learn about the things they endured until recently. Even into adulthood, my sisters never thought it important or useful to drudge up what they'd protected me from. Learning about the atrocities they endured brought up new, complicated feelings for me. Their experiences filled in a lot of the missing pieces of my memory, made my naiveté seem infantile. I am in utter awe of who these women have become despite these things, and I couldn't be more thankful for the blinds they rolled down in front of me when I was a kid. But it is now important for me to share some of those gaps in which they've filled, to share knowledge that I couldn't have had.

Andrea.

Andrea left such a long time ago, and has since separated herself from all of us. For the longest time, part of me interpreted it as abandonment, but now, I understand. Lola bore witness to a lot of the horrific abuse that Andrea endured. They were interred together, similarly how Cheryl and I were. But Andrea had it the worst of us all. She was the first born, born when Dad was still young and full of maniacal energy. Lola remembers Andrea asking her to follow her when Dad called for Andrea to come downstairs. Lola would stay quietly behind, just at the steps. Andrea found an ally in Lola, but Lola couldn't do anything to help her. Lola crept out from the stairs, undetected, and to her unimaginable horror, witnessed the sexual abuse that Andrea was subjected to. I can't even begin to articulate everything that was done to Andrea, and I won't attempt to. It's far too much for me to handle. After what

Dad did to me, I just know that Andrea endured the brunt of our father's most disgusting actions. By the time I came of age, more than twenty years later, Dad was tired, fatigued, and too sick to do the same to me. He knew he was in for a fight he couldn't finish when I pushed him away.

I had no idea as a child that my father checked himself into the Tiffin State Psychiatric Hospital on several occasions. My sisters told me that when the news came out about Andrea, Dad voluntarily admitted himself. They told me that Mom went to the hospital with a gun, held it to my dad's head, and asked him if he'd hurt Andrea. Mom asked him if Andrea was telling the truth. Of course, my dad denied everything. I don't know much of the details after that, but I do know that Andrea was made out to be a liar about everything. No one believed her. I do remember that much. I just didn't understand why back then.

I understand now. I understand why Andrea has chosen to stay away, tucked away in California. Perhaps she still thinks that no one believes her. But I *DO* believe my sister. I want her to know that. I want her to know that I understand.

Looking back, I also now understand why my sisters used to get upset with me for my dismissive behavior. Between being the youngest and being shielded by them, I was blind to a lot. More than that, I assume that I blocked a lot of things from my mind to protect myself. All I know is that my dad was a monster. I don't know how I would have dealt with all of this had I been born ten years earlier. Would I have been as strong to stand up against my father? Would I have endured much more abuse? Would Dad have done much worse to me? I can't be sure.

There are a million other things that I missed. A million things that comprise my sister's stories. A million things that I could never convey with proper justice. Things that, naively, I never expected to hear. All of my sisters remember my dad making them sit and drink alcohol with him. I suspect he did this to dull their senses or in the hopes they might pass out. Janelle has recounted watching our dad selling guns out of the front room while her and Lola also admit to having found drugs in Dad's forbidden closet. They found a brick of marijuana, a lot of pills, and some guns. They took the drugs to St. Wendelin and sold them to their peers while smoking pot and cigarettes across the street from school. Luckily, Dad never caught on.

With all of my memories and these new accounts of such appalling abuse dizzying my mind, I remind myself that the purpose of putting it all down here is to try and bring healing and love. In order to bring light and to move forward, all of this, my story, must be put out in plain sight, must be reconciled, and then given purpose. I continue to ask God to help me tackle this, to help us all find healing. To make the purpose of this convalescence be our healing.

CHAPTER THIRTEEN

my training in difference is my difference maker

Now, at the end of it all, I am a lawyer with a loving husband and two beautiful children. It has been a long and arduous road getting here, and my husband should be commended for being the insightful, patient person that he is. But even once I reached these goals, even once I attained my dreams, things didn't simply fall into place the way I imagined they would. To live happily ever after is truly the ruse of fairytales. That isn't the end to anyone's story. Certainly not mine.

Being married to David has brought me infinite happiness in life, but the residual damage of my childhood will never fully cease to exist. From time to time, it stills gnaws at our relationship, but over the years, I've had a few important revelations that have healed big parts of me. It took me a long time to stop expecting the bottom to fall out with David. I wasted so much time being suspicious of him, waiting for him to *do something*. I always felt like I needed to have a backup plan, just in case. I couldn't trust him the way that I wanted to. When things got too intense, I'd just run away. Married or not, I wouldn't let myself feel trapped. The truth, though, is that I have never been trapped by David, rather I've always been trapped by my past. I was never running away from David, but I've always been running away from myself.

I gave birth to our son, CJ, in the first year of our marriage. I'd never felt anything so amazing. For all the years I told myself that I would never give birth to interracial children for fear of what they'd go through, the moment I looked upon my son, I knew he was exactly who he was supposed to be. He was born of pure love and his life would be different than mine. I'd make sure of that.

When CJ was six months old, David and I had our first big argument as husband and wife. I couldn't tell you what it was about—didn't matter enough. Nonetheless, in the middle of our fight, I took CJ out of his swing, grabbed my purse, and dashed out to the car.

"What in the world are you doing?" David came out after me as I was strapping CJ into his car seat.

I didn't answer him directly. I just continued to mumble to myself. *He thinks he can tell me what to do. Well, he's wrong. I don't think so. I don't have to deal with this! No one gets to do this to me. No one!*

I snapped to this irrational place in my mind where I was convinced David was trying to control me. I didn't give my brain permission to do this. Fear is involuntary, and when you have been raised as volatile as I have, something in your consciousness clicks off and your defenses click on at any sign of danger, real or perceived. I yelled something rude back at David, got in the car, and sped off.

As I flew down the street, I broke out crying. I started to scream and pound on the steering wheel. I felt so disappointed, so scared that everything was being ruined with David, with our new family. *Why is it falling apart?*

My emotions were dramatic and reactionary, and frankly, uncalled for. But I couldn't see that then. In those moments, I couldn't wrangle with any reason. I'd just shut down, leave, and hate everything in the universe for having let me down again.

I pulled into the community center parking lot and laid my head on the steering wheel. I had to quit sobbing. As I drew in some deep breaths, I thought about the backseat of the Travelall. I thought about Mom. I was acting it out all over. I had become her without even knowing it. Mom always left when things got challenging, and there we were, in the backseat, confused and scared. I had been taught to do that, to run away. And while Mom needed to run, I was in different circumstances. This was just a normal argument. *What am I doing?* I looked back at CJ and realized how far I'd gone in my mind. This was a steep reaction to a minor problem.

On the drive back, I thought about the ways in which my mom lives inside of me. There are these moments when I fly off at David that are purely reactionary, knee-jerk responses. I see my mom in that. I see these fiery tinges of Mom that seep out of my mouth, sometimes no matter how hard I try to keep it closed, and David doesn't deserve that. But more deeply than a sassy attitude, there was a disturbed part of my mom that I think was instilled in all of us. We all were abused by Dad. We were all scared, and when things seem too overwhelming for me and I feel that snap coming on, I think about Mom walking down the side of the street, next to the car, refusing to get in, and I get it. Sadly, I get it.

Some of my sisters don't necessarily feel the same way when it comes to Mom, I suppose. While all challenging, all of our experiences were different so I can't dictate to any of them how they should feel. I respect whatever emotions have been created inside of them toward our mom, but I simply can't hold her accountable for the heartache in my life. My mother loved her children from a distance. She, too, built a protective barrier, which is partially what made her so mysterious when we were younger. I have to consider that seven children is a lot. That being married to my dad was a lot. And that, in different times, some things were inescapable. Is she responsible for my childhood? In part, yes. But what else can she do other than apologize? What would be good enough? I don't have a price for her to pay. I just forgive her because I know that I have required a lot of forgiveness in my life. Who am I to deny forgiveness for my mother? She doesn't owe me anything. I don't need her to acknowledge my pain or my struggle for me to heal or to feel satisfied. The only person that can heal me is God, the only person I need to answer to is God, and the only thing that can satisfy me is a relationship with Him. What's done is done and we've all hurt too much to not move on. Besides, I love my mother so much that I would do anything to protect her and will, for the rest of my life, love her unconditionally and with the upmost respect.

When our daughter Ciera was born, I couldn't stop staring at her. She was, still is, so beautiful. I promised from that day forward that if I could not do anything right, that I would always love, kiss, hug, and pray with my children every single day. So far, so good.

When I watch David with our children, I just watch in amazement of what a daddy should be. As CJ and CC grew, I was really amazed by him as a father and that grew my love for him a hundred fold. I still watch him with them and think, *Oh, that's what a dad is.* It wasn't until I got to experience this, until David showed me firsthand what it truly meant to love your children, was I able to mature enough to let our relationship evolve into what it is today. Watching David be a real father has been healing for me, and I mourn for my mother knowing that she didn't get to experience that with Dad. She had to be suspicious of him and carry guilt for the way he treated us. I wish she could've had what I have now.

Going forward, I need to share my story for all of the timid and disenfranchised little girls out there—even the ones who have grown into women now, but still struggle deep inside, so that they may find the truth too. And the truth is that nothing is unconquerable with God and the truth that lies within the Word of God. No barrier is too high and no challenge is too great. I didn't know that for a very long time.

For I can do everything through Christ, who gives me strength.
Philippians 4:13

Sharing my story has granted me freedom like I've never known and I wish I'd done it sooner. Part of finding success and the career I always dreamt of has been reliant on my ability to be transparent with others and to connect with them through my story—ironically, the last thing I ever thought that I needed to do to find not only success, but healing. Having worked only five months at a Fortune 500 company in Toledo, the CLO, Steve Krull, asked if I was interested in leading their United Way campaign—one of their biggest fundraisers. Of course, I accepted, bright eyed and ready to tackle the challenge.

He explained to me that he wanted to create what he called a "real life campaign." He wanted to put faces to real life stories so that personal connections could be made in a more inspiring way. I was totally on board, excited to be a part of it.

Then he said this:

"The story starts with us, Diana. What's your story?"

I was speechless. I looked up from my notes and stared at him, dumbfounded. I'd never told anyone anything. No one knew about my life, about my brother, about my father—no one besides David and that old therapist. I kept things under pretty tight lock and key so this question terrified me. *How am I going to answer this?*

I stuttered to buy time.

"What do you mean?" I asked.

"Have you had any tragedy in your life? Anything you've had to overcome? You know, problems that you've battled to get here?" he looked at me for a response. "Or, hey, maybe life's been pretty good to you? If so, you can share that too."

My hands were sweating. I had cotton mouth. I couldn't stop licking the roof of my mouth and the front of my teeth. *Should I lie?* Then the nausea set in. I took a sip of water, a deep breath, and looked out the window to escape the room for a minute. I looked over the flowing Maumee River and thought about what I should say, trying to clear my head. As I watched the water trip over rocks, I started to calm down a bit. There was something different about this moment, something surreal blanketing over it. I felt like God was taking the burden out of my chest and giving me the permission to talk. He was giving me reassurance. I could feel that. I knew I could be honest. I just needed a minute before I got started.

Just to be sure, I looked down at my hands and said to Steve, "You really want to know about my life?"

"Absolutely. This starts with you."

I shook my head and bit my lip.

"Okay," I looked at him.

A play button switched on inside of me. I started off slow, but before long, I was rattling on about my deepest and most difficult trauma. My voice stopped cracking, stopped wavering at all. I told him everything from my first memory to the most recent. I told him about Dad, about my sisters, and about our house, about school, and about discrimination. I told him about Damon and about the hardships I had in college. I told him everything plus how I felt about everything.

Steve sat there, speechless.

I cried right there in his office. I cried all over his office chair like I had paid for a therapy session. I soaked my shirt and smeared tears all up and down my arms. I was a mess.

"What an amazing story, Diana," Steve leaned forward.

But I had to excuse myself and run to the bathroom.

Why did you tell him that? What did you just do? The voice in my head was screaming. I thought for sure I'd get demoted, that he would immediately revoke the United Way campaign from me. I stood in the bathroom, trying to compose myself, wiping off my face with wet paper towels. I couldn't believe what I'd done.

Luckily, the opposite happened. I kept the campaign and when I returned to his office, the CLO simply looked at me and said, "Now I know why I chose you."

Vulnerability saved me. The one thing that I spent my entire life trying not to be, now opened a giant opportunity for me.

In the days following, I felt better than ever. I'd given away my secret to someone and surprisingly, it felt really good. There was a lighter feeling about my body. Talking about my past breathed new life into me and I knew then that I'd found my cure. I had to use my story, not hide it. That is my purpose.

During the United Way campaign, I connected with so many amazing people. I can't say that telling my story ever became much easier, but I never again felt embarrassed about doing it. Admitting that certain things from my past hurt me felt powerful. Those things no longer owned me. They had no power over me anymore. I was no longer accountable to pain or grief or disappointment.

When I started to share, I started to thrive. My whole world began to blossom with opportunity while I healed at the same time. There's power in truth, and sharing my truth completely changed my trajectory from teetering on despair to running full force into my dreams. From this sprang my life's mission—to promote healthy change for women everywhere. It never gets easy, but if I've learned anything at all, it's that we are never in the future. My future is always opening and my job is to work on myself so that I can help others to be better.

What followed the United Way campaign was nothing short of amazing. One day, while running on the treadmill, I was reading *Health Magazine*. There was a contest, The Face of Health, and it was titled, "Do you believe you are the face of health?"

Something about this opportunity set off alarms in my head. *Yes.* After everything, I learned the importance of not just physical health but emotional, psychological, and spiritual health too. I had come so far—farther than most people ever have to go. *Yes, I am the face of health.*

I submitted to the contest and was chosen among four other women to express why I embodied the face of health in their October, 2004 edition. My long journey brought me to this victory. I had traveled through vulnerability and arrived at authenticity, and this was my opportunity to share that journey with others. When the magazine contacted me to notify me that I'd won, they said I'd be flown to New York City for a photoshoot for the article spread. My mind immediately shot to Damon. This was the kiss of God. This was Him saying that I was now meant to complete my journey—to take that trip, and to find closure in the fact that now, ten years after my cancelled NYC trip, that it was finally time.

Maintaining a healthy lifestyle became increasingly important to me and my quest for knowledge led me to the Institute for Integrative Nutrition. I wanted to help others and I thought that perhaps IIN could provide me with even greater tools to do that. I felt such a strong pull to IIN. I couldn't explain it adequately to David or really make him understand. I just simply knew that going there was the right next step for me.

I flew to Manhattan for a weekend once every month for classes. From the moment I walked into IIN, I knew I had found my people, so to speak. I felt free there—free to live my purpose, free to learn and absorb everything, free to follow my journey. Everyone at IIN was free-spirited, longing for purpose, and reaching out to serve others. The atmosphere buzzed with intention and though the travel to New York every month was taxing, I reveled in my decision to attend IIN. It was perfect.

There is a particular moment in my time at IIN that helped shape my direction. IIN founder, Joshua Rosenthal, was addressing our class when he asked, "Who out of this group thinks that they are a good public speaker?" Of course, I was waving my hand so high that I think he was scared of me. In fact, he looked right at me before looking away.

"Anyone? Anyone think you can do this?" Joshua continued to scan the room.

I almost ripped my own arm off waving it so hard. He reluctantly called on me. I ran up to the front like I had been called up on *The Price is Right*.

"Okay," Joshua looked at me "take two to three minutes and talk about what you see in this room. What you say should inspire us."

I nodded.

"On your mark, get set, go."

I took off. I was running the 400-yard dash. I spoke so clearly, so deeply, and with such compassion that I didn't hear him say "time" the first time. I had wings. I was alive. I was in my element, and before I knew it, a room full of people roared, cheered, screamed, clapped and stood. I was flying again. Up above it all. Only this time, it wasn't a dream.

I was successful at IIN and for graduation, Joshua asked me to prepare a speech. I was honored. When I spoke at graduation, I was greeted with another standing ovation. In the midst of all the clapping, Joshua put his hand on my back and whispered in my ear, "Get used to this. This is what you were meant to do."

For two years after that day, Joshua asked me to come back and speak to the students. My purpose was growing all of the time.

I know that my checkered past causes doubt in some people's minds as to who I am. I'm certain that there is a fair amount to say about the person that I was. But I am no longer that person and God has prepared me for rejection, criticism, and a life of earthly unacceptance.

This means that anyone who belongs to Christ has become a new person.
The old life is gone; a new life has begun! 2 Corinthians 5:17

I am not supposed to look to others in order for me to accept myself, and neither should anyone else. God wants me to be bold in my difference and to share it in a powerful and mighty way despite the rejection, despite the ridicule, despite the doubt, and despite the skepticism that is sure to come. My journey requires that my life have a ripple effect long after my time on Earth.

God has a way of preparing your purpose for you. Although it may seem that I spent much of my life swaddled by pain and enveloped by darkness, finding my way through is the only thing that could've led to who I am today. For that, I am grateful. When you are in the trenches, when the world around you seems cruel, when you feel completely alone, you also find your strength. I can understand why people might think I should hate where I come from, or that I should be resentful for the things that have happened to me, but those things compose who I am. For every ounce of heartache that I've endured, I have a pound of love to give to another young woman, struggling in the dark, wading in the pain. For every loss I've felt—of Damon, of my youth, of my integrity, of my sanity, of even my father—I have unbounding support to offer to those who might feel like their drowning alone. Nothing that's happened in my life has happened without purpose. My purpose is to serve, and my ability to do that solely rests on the wealth of pain that I have experienced. This is why no one should ever give up. This is why no one should ever hate who they are, or who they've become at the hands of difficult circumstances. I am grateful for it all. I am thankful, for I am a beacon now, signaling those swimming in the waters of despair to shore.

My training in difference is my difference maker.

Diana Patton, 36

Corporate diversity leader in
Toledo, Ohio

ON LIVING HEALTHY: "After years of working at a job that required lots of travel, I got my priorities straight and accepted a job closer to home. Evenings are family time, so I set my alarm for 5:15 every morning and usually exercise before work. Sometimes I throw on sneakers and go for a run or do an exercise video in my pajamas. I strive to cook every night—mostly healthy meals, though we occasionally have pizza or a chocolate dessert. It's not living if you don't give yourself treats."

ON SURVIVING SETBACKS: "Ten years ago, my youngest brother committed suicide. The only way I could deal with the tragedy was to draw on my faith in order to create something positive from it. So I founded a high school scholarship in his honor. Kids ostracized him, so this award is for the child who goes over to talk to that kid standing alone on the playground, the one nobody wants to play with."

ON SELF-IMAGE: "I modeled professionally for 10 years, but I feel more beautiful today because I'm happier."

Diana's secrets
for inner & outer beauty

HIGHLIGHT YOUR BEST FEATURE with makeup. "I play up my lips with liner and colored gloss—M.A.C and Bobbi Brown are my favorites—and keep everything else on my face understated. That way my makeup never looks overdone."

THINK POSITIVE. "A negative attitude shows on your face, in the way you walk, the way you speak—everything."

Go to Health.com and click on "Beauty" for more behind-the-scenes info and photos of our winners.

"Real living means learning to accept yourself—stretch marks, self-doubts, and all."

OCTOBER 20

Diana, The Face of Health, Health Magazine, October, 2004.

Diana, Women's Only Triathalon & Di-Tri Race, July 29, 2009.

Diana and her mother, present day. Diana's mother, Joni, still lives in Diana's childhood home. This photo was taken in the front room. One day, Diana hopes to buy her mom a new home.

Diana and David's family, present day.

Don't be afraid, for I am with you. Don't be discouraged, for I am your God. I will strengthen you and help you. I will hold you up with my victorious right hand.

Isaiah 41:10

CPSIA information can be obtained at www.ICGtesting.com
Printed in the USA
BVOW06s1158130616

451829BV00013B/76/P